Bem-vindo!

Just Enough **Portuguese**

D. L. Ellis, K. Sandeman McLaughlin

Pronunciation **Dr. J. Baldwin**

PASSPORT BOOKS
a division of *NTC Publishing Group*
Lincolnwood, Illinois USA

The publishers would like to thank the Portuguese National Tourist Office for their help in the preparation of this book

1993 Printing

This edition first published in 1983 by Passport Books,
a division of NTC Publishing Group,
4255 West Touhy Avenue,
Lincolnwood (Chicago), Illinois 60646-1975 U.S.A.
Originally published by Pan Books, © D.L. Ellis and
K. Sandeman McLaughlin, 1981.
Manufactured in the United States of America.

2 3 4 5 6 7 8 9 0 AG 9

Contents

Using the phrase book

- This phrase book is designed to help you get by in Portugal and Brazil, to get what you want or need. It concentrates on the simplest but most effective way you can express these needs in an unfamiliar language.
- The CONTENTS on p. 5 gives you a good idea of which section to consult for the phrase you need.
- The index on p. 153 gives more detailed information about where to look for your phrase.
- When you have found the right page you will be given:
  either – the exact phrase
  or   – help in making up a suitable sentence
  and   – help to get the pronunciation right
- The English sentences in **bold type** will be useful for you in a variety of different situations, so they are worth learning by heart. (See also DO IT YOURSELF, p. 143).
- Wherever possible you will find help in understanding what Portuguese-speaking people are saying to *you*, in reply to your questions.
- If you want to practice the basic nuts and bolts of the language further, look at the DO IT YOURSELF section starting p. 145.
- Note especially these three sections:
  Everyday expressions p. 12
  Shop talk p. 56
  Public signs p. 121
  You are sure to want to refer to them most frequently
- Once abroad, remember to make good use of the local tourist offices (see p. 25)
  US addresses:
  Portuguese National Tourist Office
  548 Fifth Avenue
  New York, NY 10036
  (212) 354-4403

  Brazilian Consulate Office
  630 Fifth Avenue
  Room 2720
  New York, NY 10111
  (212) 757-3080

A note on the pronunciation system

In traveler's phrase books there is usually a pronunciation section which tries to teach English-speaking tourists how to correctly pronounce the language of the country they are visiting. This is based on the belief that in order to be understood, the speaker must have an accurate, authentic accent – that he must pronounce every last word letter-perfectly.

The authors of this book, on the other hand, wanted to devise a workable and usable pronunciation system. So they had to face the fact it is absolutely impossible for an average speaker of English who has no technical training in phonetics and phonetic transcription systems (which includes 98% of all the users of this book!) to reproduce the sounds of a foreign language with perfect accuracy, just from reading a phonetic transcription, cold – no prior background in the language. We also believe that you don't have to have perfect pronunciation in order to make yourself understood in a foreign country. After all, natives you run into will take into account that you are foreigners, and visitors, and more than likely they will feel gratified by your efforts to communicate and will probably go out of their way to try to understand you. They may even help you, and correct you, in a friendly manner. We have found, also, that visitors to a foreign country are not usually concerned with perfect pronunciation – they just want to get their message across, to communicate!

With this in mind, we have designed a pronunciation system which is of the utmost simplicity to use. This system does not attempt to give an accurate – but also problematical and tedious – representation of the sound system of the language, but instead uses common sound and letter combinations in English which are the closest to the sounds in the foreign language. In this way, the sentences transcribed for pronunciation should be read as naturally as possible, as if they were ordinary English. In no way does the user have to attempt to make the words sound "foreign." So, while to yourselves you will sound as if you are speaking ordinary English – or at least making ordinary English sounds – you will at the same time be making yourselves understood in another language. And, as the saying goes, practice makes perfect, so it is probably a good idea to repeat aloud to yourselves several times the phrases you think you are going to use, before you actually use them. This will give you greater confidence, and will also help in making yourself understood.

In Portuguese, it is important to stress or emphasize the syllables in *italics*, just as you would if we were to take as an English example: *Little* Jack *Horner* sat in the *corner*. Here we have ten syllables but only four stresses.

Of course you may enjoy trying to pronounce a foreign language as well as possible, and the present system is a good way to start. However, since it uses only the sounds of English, you will very soon need to depart from it as you imitate the sounds you hear the native speaker produce and relate them to the spelling of the other language.

Boa sorte!
b*o*a sort

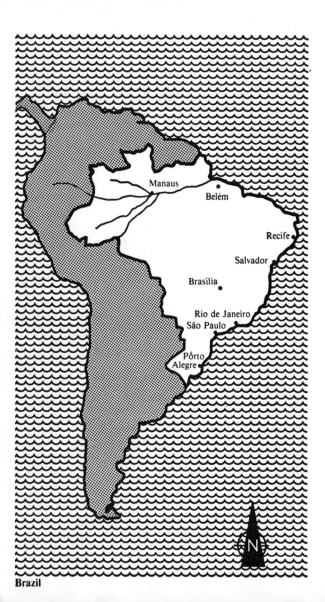

Manaus

Belém

Recife

Salvador

Brasília

Rio de Janeiro
São Paulo

Pôrto
Alegre

N

Brazil

GRACIOSA

TERCEIRA

FAIAL SÃO JORGE

PICO

SÃO MIGUEL

STA MARIA

PORTO SANTO

MADEIRA

CORVO

FLORES

Spain

Porto

Coimbra

Lisbon

Faro

Portugal

Everyday expressions

[See also 'Shop talk', p. 56]

Hello	**Olá**
	olah
Good morning ⎤	**Bom dia**
Good day ⎦	bom dee-a
Good afternoon	**Boa tarde**
	boa tard
Good night	**Boa noite**
	boa noyt
Goodbye	**Adeus**
	adeh-oosh
See you later	**Até logo**
	ateh log-oo
Yes	**Sim**
	seem
Please	**Por favor**
	poor favor
Yes, please	**Sim, por favor**
	seem poor favor
Great!	**Óptimo!**
	o-teemoo
Thank you	**Obrigado/a***
	obreegah-doo/a
Thank you very much	**Muito obrigado/a***
	moo-eetoo obreegah-doo/a
That's right	**Exactamente**
	eezatament
No	**Não**
	nown
No thanks	**Não obrigado/a***
	nown obreegah-doo/a
I disagree	**Não concordo**
	nown concordoo
Excuse me ⎤	**Desculpe**
Sorry ⎦	deshcoolp
Don't mention it ⎤	**Não tem de quê**
That's OK ⎦	nown taim der keh

*First alternative for men, second for women

That's good / I like it	**Está bem** shtah baim
That's no good / I don't like it	**Não está bem** nown shtah baim
I know	**Eu sei** *e*h-oo say
I don't know	**Eu não sei** *e*h-oo nown say
It doesn't matter	**Não faz mal** nown f*a*sh mal
Where's the toilet, please?	**Onde é a casa de banho, por favor?** awnd *e*h a c*a*h-za der b*ai*n-yoo poor fav*o*r
How much is that? [*point*]	**Quanto custa?** kwantoo c*oo*shta
Is the service included?	**O serviço está incluído?** oo serv*ee*ssoo shtah eencloo-*ee*doo
Do you speak English?	**Fala inglês?** F*a*h-la eenglesh
I'm sorry . . .	**Desculpe . . .** deshc*oo*lp . . .
I don't speak Portuguese	**não falo português** nown f*a*h-loo poortoog*e*sh
I only speak a little Portuguese	**só falo um pouco português** s*o*h f*a*h-loo oom p*a*wkoo poortoog*e*sh
I don't understand	**não compreendo** nown compree-*e*ndoo
Please can you . . .	**Por favor, pode . . .** poor fav*o*r pod . . .
repeat that?	**repetir?** rep-et-*ee*r
speak more slowly?	**falar mais devagar?** fal*a*r m*a*h-eesh devag*a*r
write it down?	**escrever?** shkrev*ai*r
What is this called in Portuguese? [*point*]	**Como se diz isto em português?** c*o*moo ser deesh *ee*shtoo aim poortoog*e*sh

Crossing the border

ESSENTIAL INFORMATION

- Don't waste time just before you leave rehearsing what you're going to say to the border officials – the chances are that you won't have to say anything at all, especially if you travel by air.
- It's more useful to check that you have your documents handy for the journey: passport, tickets, money, travellers' cheques, insurance documents, driving licence and car registration documents.
- Look out for these signs:
  ALFÂNDEGA (customs)
  FRONTEIRA (border)
  POLÍCIA ALFANDEGÁRIA ⎤ (frontier police)
  POLÍCIA ADUANEIRA ⎦
  [*For further signs and notices see p. 121*]
- You may well be asked routine questions by the customs officials [*see below*]. If you have to give personal details see 'Meeting people', p. 16. The most important answer to know is 'Nothing': **Nada** (n*ah*-da).

ROUTINE QUESTIONS

Passport?	**Passaporte?**
	passap*or*t
Insurance?	**Seguro?**
	seg*oo*roo
Registration document? (logbook)	**Livrete?**
	leevr*et*
Ticket, please	**O bilhete, por favor**
	oo beel-y*et* poor fav*or*
Have you anything to declare?	**Tem alguma coisa a declarar?**
	taim alg*oo*ma c*oy*-za a declar*ar*
Where are you going?	**Para onde vai?**
	p*a*ra awnd v*ah*-ee
How long are you staying?	**Quanto tempo fica?**
	kw*a*ntoo t*ai*mpoo f*ee*ka
Where have you come from?	**De onde vem?**
	der awnd vaim

You may also have to fill in forms which ask for:

surname	**apelido**
first name	**(primeiros) nomes**
maiden name	**nome de solteira**
place of birth	**local de nascimento**
date of birth	**data de nascimento**
address	**morada**
nationality	**nacionalidade**
profession	**profissão**
passport number	**número do passaporte**
issued at	**emitido em**
signature	**assinatura**

Meeting people

[See also 'Everyday expressions', p. 12]

Breaking the ice

Hello
Olá
olah

Good morning
Bom dia
bom dee-a

How are you?
Como está?
comoo shtah

Pleased to meet you
Muito prazer
moo-eetoo prazair

I am here . . .
Estou aqui . . .
shtaw akee . . .

  on holiday
de férias
der fairee-ash

  on business
em negócios
aim negossee-oosh

Can I offer you . . .
Posso lhe oferecer . . .
possoo l-yeh ofresair . . .

  a drink?
uma bebida?
ooma bebeeda

  a cigarette?
um cigarro?
oom seegarroo

  a cigar?
um charuto?
oom sharootoo

Are you staying long?
Fica por muito tempo?
feeka poor moo-eetoo taimpoo

Name

What is your name?
Como se chama?
comoo ser shah-ma

My name is . . .
Chamo-me . . .
shamoo-meh . . .

Family

Are you married?	**É casado/a***
	eh caz*a*h-doo/a
I am . . .	**Sou . . .**
	saw . . .
married	**casado/a***
	caz*a*h-doo/a
single	**solteiro/a***
	solt*ay*-roo/a
This is . . .	**Apresento-lhe . . .**
	apres*e*ntoo l-yeh . . .
my wife	**a minha mulher**
	a m*ee*n-ya mool-y*ai*r
my husband	**o meu marido**
	oo meh-oo mar*ee*doo
my son	**o meu filho**
	oo meh-oo f*ee*l-yoo
my daughter	**a minha filha**
	a m*ee*n-ya f*ee*l-ya
my boyfriend	**o meu namorado**
	oo meh-oo namoor*a*h-doo
my girlfriend	**a minha namorada**
	a m*ee*n-ya namoor*a*h-da
my (male) colleague	**o meu colega**
	oo meh-oo kool*e*g-a
my (female) colleague	**a minha colega**
	a m*ee*n-ya kool*e*g-a
Do you have any children?	**Tem filhos?**
	taim f*ee*l-yoosh
I have . . .	**Tenho . . .**
	t*a*in-yoo . . .
one daughter	**uma filha**
	*oo*ma f*ee*l-ya
one son	**um filho**
	oom f*ee*l-yoo
two daughters	**duas filhas**
	d*oo*-ash f*ee*l-yash
three sons	**três filhos**
	tresh f*ee*l-yoosh
No, I haven't any children	**Não, não tenho filhos**
	nown, nown t*a*in-yoo f*ee*l-yoosh

*First alternative for men, second for women.

Where you live

Are you . . .	**Você é . . .**
	vosseh eh
Portuguese?	**português/portuguesa?***
	poortoogesh/poortoogeza
Brazilian?	**brasileiro/a?***
	brazeelayroo/a
I am . . .	**Sou . . .**
	saw . . .
American	**americano/a***
	americanoo/a
English	**inglês/inglesa***
	eenglesh/eenglez-a

[*For other nationalities, see p. 134*]

I live . . .	**Moro . . .**
	moh-roo . . .
in London	**em Londres**
	aim londresh
in England	**em Inglaterra**
	aim eenglatairra
in the north	**no norte**
	noo nort
in the south	**no sul**
	noo sool
in the east	**no este**
	noo esht
in the west	**no oeste**
	noo oh-aisht
in the centre	**no centro**
	noo sentroo

*First alternative for men, second for women.

For the businessman and woman

I'm from . . . (firm's name)	**Sou de . . .** saw der . . .
I have an appointment with . . .	**Tenho uma entrevista marcada com . . .** tain-yoo ooma entreveeshta marcah-da com . . .
May I speak to . . . ?	**Posso falar com . . . ?** possoo falar com . . .
This is my card	**Este é o meu cartão** esht eh oo meh-oo cartown
I'm sorry I'm late	**Desculpe chegar atrasado/a*** deshcoolp shegar atrazah-doo/a
Can I fix another appointment?	**Posso marcar outra entrevista?** possoo marcar awtra entreveeshta
I'm staying at the (Park) hotel	**Estou no Hotel (Parque)** shtaw noo otel (park)
I'm staying in the (Rua Augusta)	**Estou na (Rua Augusta)** shtaw nah (roo-a ah-oogooshta)

*First alternative for men, second for women

Asking the way

ESSENTIAL INFORMATION

• Keep a look out for all these place names as you will find them on shops, maps and notices.

WHAT TO SAY

Excuse me, please **Com licença por favor**
com leesen-sa poor favor

How do I get . . . **Para ir . . .**
para eer . . .

to Lisbon? **a Lisboa?**
a leeshboo-a

to Rua Augusta? **à Rua Augusta?**
ah roo-a ah-oogooshta

to the (hotel) Ritz? **ao (hotel) Ritz?**
ah-oo (otel) reetz

to the airport? **ao aeroporto?**
ah-oo airoh-portoo

to the beach? **à praia?**
ah prah-ya

to the bus station? **à estação de camionetas?**
ah shtassown der cam-yoonet-ash

to the historic site? **ao lugar histórico?**
ah-oo loogar shtoreekoo

to the market? **ao mercado?**
ah-oo maircah-doo

to the police station? **à esquadra?**
ah shkwah-dra

to the port? **ao porto?**
ah-oo portoo

to the post office? **aos correios?**
ah-oosh cooray-oosh

to the railway station? **à estação (de comboios)?**
ah shtassown (der comboy-oosh)

to the sports stadium? **ao estádio desportivo?**
ah-oo shtah-dee-oo deshpoorteevoo

to the tourist information office?	**ao centro de informações turísticas?**
	ah-oo sentroo der eenfoor-mass*oy*nsh tooreesh-teecash
to the town centre?	**ao centro (da cidade)?**
	ah-oo sentroo da seed*a*d
to the town hall?	**à câmara municipal?**
	ah c*a*mera mooneeseep*a*l
Excuse me, please	**Com licença por favor**
	com leesen-sa poor fav*o*r
Is there . . . near by?	**Há . . . aqui perto?**
	ah . . . ak*ee* p*a*irtoo
an art gallery	**uma galeria de arte**
	*oo*ma galer*ee*-a der art
a baker's	**uma padaria**
	*oo*ma padayr*ee*-a
a bank	**um banco**
	oom b*a*ncoo
a bar	**um bar**
	oom b*a*r
a botanical garden	**um jardim botânico**
	oom jard*ee*m boot*a*n-icoo
a bus stop	**uma paragem de autocarros**
	*oo*ma par*a*jaim der ah-ootoh-carroosh
a butcher's	**um talho**
	oom t*a*l-yoo
a café	**um café**
	oom caf*e*h
a cake shop	**uma pastelaria**
	*oo*ma pashtelar*ee*-a
a campsite	**um parque de campismo**
	oom park der camp*ee*j-moo
a car park	**um parking**
	oom p*a*rking
a change bureau	**um banco com câmbio**
	oom b*a*ncoo com c*a*mbee-oo
a chemist's	**uma farmácia**
	*oo*ma farm*a*h-see-a
a church	**uma igreja**
	*oo*ma eegr*a*y-ja

Is there . . . near by?	**Há . . . aqui perto?**
	ah . . . ak*ee* p*ai*rtoo
a cinema	**um cinema**
	oom seen*e*m-a
a delicatessen	**uma charcutaria**
	*oo*ma sharcoota*ree*-a
a dentist's	**um dentista**
	oom dent*ee*shta
a department store	**um armazém**
	oom armaz*ai*m
a disco	**uma discoteca**
	*oo*ma deesh-coot*e*h-ca
a doctor's surgery	**um consultório médico**
	oom consoolt*o*ree-oo m*e*dicoo
a dry-cleaner's	**uma tinturaria**
	*oo*ma teentoora*ree*-a
a fishmonger's	**uma peixaria**
	*oo*ma paysha*ree*-a
a garage (for repairs)	**uma garagem**
	*oo*ma gar*a*jaim
a greengrocer's	**uma frutaria**
	*oo*ma froota*ree*-a
a grocer's	**uma mercearia**
	*oo*ma mersee-ar*ee*-a
a hairdresser's	**um cabeleireiro**
	oom cab-el-ay-r*a*yroo
a hardware shop	**uma loja de ferragens**
	*oo*ma l*o*ja der ferr*a*jaimsh
a hospital	**um hospital**
	oom oshpeet*a*l
a hotel	**um hotel**
	oom ot*e*l
an ice-cream parlour	**uma gelataria**
	*oo*ma jelatar*ee*-a
a laundry	**uma lavandaria**
	*oo*ma lavandar*ee*-a
a museum	**um museu**
	oom mooz*e*h-oo
a newsagent's	**uma papelaria**
	*oo*ma papelar*ee*-a
a night club	**uma 'boîte'**
	*oo*ma boo-*a*t

a park	**um parque**
	oom park
a petrol station	**uma bomba de gasolina**
	ooma bomba der gazooleena
a post box	**uma caixa do correio**
	ooma kah-eesha doo corrayoo
a public garden	**um jardim público**
	oom jardeem pooblicoo
a public telephone	**uma cabine telefónica**
	ooma cah-been telefoneeca
a public toilet	**uma casa de banho pública**
	ooma cah-za der bain-yoo pooblica
a restaurant	**um restaurante**
	oom reshtah-oorant
a snack bar	**um snack-bar/um café**
	oom snak-bar/oom cafeh
a sports ground	**um campo desportivo**
	oom campoo deshpoorteevoo
a supermarket	**um supermercado**
	oom supermaircah-doo
a sweet shop	**uma confeitaria**
	ooma confaytaree-a
a swimming pool	**uma piscina**
	ooma peesh-seena
a taxi stand	**um parque de taxis**
	oom park der taxeesh
a theatre	**um teatro**
	oom tee-atroo
a tobacconist's	**uma tabacaria**
	ooma tabacaree-a
a travel agent's	**uma agência de viagens**
	ooma ajensia der vee-ajainsh
a youth hostel	**uma pousada de juventude**
	ooma pawssah-da der jooventood
a zoo	**um jardim zoológico**
	oom jardeem zoolojicoo

DIRECTIONS

- Asking where a place is, or if a place is near by, is one thing; making sense of the answer is another.
- Here are some of the most important key directions and replies.

Left/Right	**Esquerda/Direita** shkairda/deerayta
Straight on	**Sempre em frente** sempr aim frent
There	**Ali** alee
First left/right	**Primeira à esquerda/direita** preemayra ah shkairda/deerayta
Second left/right	**Segunda à esquerda/direita** segoonda ah shkairda/deerayta
At the crossroads	**No cruzamento** noo croozamentoo
At the traffic lights	**Nas luzes (nos semáforos)** nash loozesh (noosh semah-foroosh)
At the roundabout	**No redondelo** noo redondel-oo
At the level-crossing	**Na passagem de nível** na passajaim der neevel
It's near/far	**É perto/longe** eh pairtoo/lawnj
One kilometre	**Um quilómetro** oom keelometroo
Two kilometres	**Dois quilómetros** doysh keelometroosh
Five minutes . . .	**Cinco minutos . . .** seencoo meenootoosh . . .
on foot/by car	**a pé/de carro** a peh/der carroo
Take . . .	**Apanhe . . .** a-pan-ye . . .
the bus	**o autocarro** oo ah-ootoh-carroo
the train	**o comboio** oo comboy-oo
the tram	**o eléctrico** oo eeletricoo
the underground [*For public transport, p. 112*]	**o metropolitano** oo metroopoo-leetan-oo

The tourist information office

ESSENTIAL INFORMATION

- Written and verbal information is available from the Directorate-General for Tourism and from the Tourist Posts to be found throughout Portugal, and from the Brazilian offices of tourism.
- Look for these words:
  DIRECÇÃO GERAL DE TURISMO
  TURISMO
- Local tourism bodies provide local and regional information.
- These offices offer you free information in the form of leaflets, foldouts, brochures, lists and plans.
- You may have to pay for some types of documents but this is not usual.
- For finding a tourist office, see p. 20.

WHAT TO SAY

Please, have you got . . .	**Por favor, tem . . .** poor favor taim . . .
a plan of the town?	**um mapa da cidade?** oom mah-pa da seedad
a list of events?	**uma lista de acontecimentos?** ooma leeshta der acontessee-mentoosh
a list of hotels?	**uma lista de hotéis?** ooma leeshta der otaysh
a list of campsites?	**uma lista de parques de campismo?** ooma leeshta der parkesh der campeejmo
a list of restaurants?	**uma lista de restaurantes?** ooma leeshta der reshtah-oorantesh
a list of coach excursions?	**uma lista de excursões de camioneta?** ooma leeshta der eshkoorsoynsh der cam-yoonet-a
a leaflet on the town?	**um panfleto sobre a cidade?** oom pamflet-oo sawbr a seedad
a leaflet on the region?	**um panfleto sobre a região?** oom pamflet-oo sawbr a rejee-own

Please, have you got . . .	**Por favor, tem . . .** poor favor taim . . .
a railway timetable?	**um horário de comboios?** oom or*ah*-ree-oo der comb*oy*-oosh
a bus timetable?	**um horário de autocarros?** oom or*ah*-ree-oo der ah-ooto- c*a*rroosh
In English, please	**Em inglês, por favor** aim eengl*esh* poor fav*o*r
How much do I owe you?	**Quanto lhe devo?** kwantoo l-yeh d*e*v-oo
Can you recommend . . .	**Pode recomendar-me . . .** pod recoomend*a*r-meh . . .
a cheap hotel?	**um hotel barato?** oom ot*e*l bar*a*too
a cheap restaurant?	**um restaurante barato?** oom resht*ah*-oorant bar*a*too
Can you make a booking for me?	**Pode fazer-me uma reserva?** pod faz*ai*r-meh *oo*ma rez*ai*rva

LIKELY ANSWERS

You need to understand when the answer is 'No'. You should be able to tell by the assistant's facial expression, tone of voice and gesture; but there are some language clues, such as:

No	**Não** nown
I'm sorry	**Desculpe** deshc*oo*lp
I don't have a list of campsites	**Não tenho uma lista de parques de campismo** nown t*ai*n-yoo *oo*ma l*ee*shta der p*a*rkesh der campe*e*jmoo
I haven't got any left	**Já não tenho nenhuns** jah nown t*ai*n-yoo nen-y*oo*nsh
It's free	**É de graça** eh der gr*a*ssa

Accommodation

Hotel

ESSENTIAL INFORMATION

- If you want hotel-type accommodation, all the following words in
  capital letters are worth looking for on name boards:
  HOTEL
  MOTEL
  PENSÃO (boarding house)
  ESTALAGEM (quality inn)
  POUSADA (state-owned inns often housed in historic buildings,
  castles, palaces and convents)

Remember that:

- A list of hotels in the town or district can usually be obtained
  from the local tourist information office [*see p. 25*].
- Unlisted hotels are usually cheaper and probably almost as good
  as listed hotels.
- Not all hotels provide meals, apart from breakfast. (A **PENSÃO**
  always provides meals.)
- The cost is displayed in the room itself, so you can check it when
  having a look around before agreeing to stay.
- The displayed cost is for the room itself, per night and not per
  person.
- Breakfast usually consists of strong coffee with milk, or tea with
  no milk unless otherwise requested, fresh bread or croissants,
  butter and jam.
- On arrival, you will be asked to complete a registration document
  and the receptionist will want to see your passport.
- Tip porters, waiters and chambermaids.
- The Directorate-General for Tourism publishes a *Tourist
  Accommodation Guide* which contains all the basic information
  on hotel establishments and tourist developments and apartments.
- Finding a hotel, see. p. 20.

WHAT TO SAY

I have a booking	**Tenho uma reserva** ta*in*-yoo *oo*ma reza*i*rva
Have you any vacancies, please?	**Tem quartos livres, por favor?** taim kwart*oo*sh l*ee*vresh poor fav*o*r
Can I book a room?	**Posso reservar um quarto?** p*o*ssoo reza*i*rvar oom kw*a*rtoo
It's for . . .	**É para . . .** eh p*a*ra . . .
one person	**uma pessoa** *oo*ma ps*aw*-a
two people [*For numbers, see p. 126*]	**duas pessoas** d*oo*-ash ps*aw*-ash
It's for . . .	**É para . . .** eh p*a*ra . . .
one night	**uma noite** *oo*ma noyt
two nights	**duas noites** d*oo*-ash noytsh
one week	**uma semana** *oo*ma sem*ah*-na
two weeks	**duas semanas** d*oo*-ash sem*ah*-nash
I would like . . .	**Queria . . .** ker*ee*-a . . .
a room	**um quarto** oom kw*a*rtoo
two rooms	**dois quartos** doysh kw*a*rtoosh
with a single bed	**com uma cama singela** com *oo*ma c*ah*-ma seenjela
with two single beds	**com duas camas separadas** com d*oo*-ash c*ah*-mash separ*ah*-dash
with a double bed	**com uma cama de casal** com *oo*ma c*ah*-ma der caz*a*l
with a toilet	**com retrete** com retr*e*t
with a bathroom	**com casa de bar ho** com c*ah*-za der b*ai*n-yoo
with a shower	**com duche** com d*oo*sh

with a cot	**com uma cama de bébé**
	com *oo*ma *ca*h-ma der beh-beh
with a balcony	**com varanda**
	com var*a*nda
I would like . . .	**Queria . . .**
	ker*ee*-a . . .
full board	**pensão completa**
	pens*ow*n compl*e*ta
half board	**meia pensão**
	m*a*y-a pens*ow*n
bed and breakfast	**dormida e pequeno almoço**
	doorm*ee*da ee pek*e*noo alm*a*wssoo
Do you serve meals?	**Servem refeições?**
	s*a*irvaim refay-s*oy*nsh
At what time is . . .	**A que horas é . . .**
	a ker *o*rash eh . . .
breakfast?	**o pequeno almoço?**
	oo pek*e*noo alm*a*wssoo
lunch?	**o almoço?**
	oo alm*a*wssoo
dinner?	**o jantar?**
	oo jant*a*r
How much is it?	**Quanto custa?**
	kw*a*ntoo c*oo*shta
Can I look at the room?	**Posso ver o quarto?**
	p*o*ssoo vair oo kw*a*rtoo
I'd prefer a room . . .	**Preferia um quarto . . .**
	prefer*ee*-a oom kw*a*rtoo . . .
at the front/at the back	**à frente/atrás**
	ah fr*e*nt/atr*a*sh
OK. I'll take it	**Está bem. Fico com ele**
	sht*a*h baim f*ee*coo com el
No thanks, I won't take it	**Não obrigado/a, não o quero***
	n*ow*n obreeg*a*h-doo/a n*ow*n oo keh-roo
The key to number (10), please	**A chave do número (dez), por favor**
	a sh*a*hv doo n*oo*meroo (desh) poor fav*o*r

*First alternative for men, second for women

Please, may I have . . .   **Pode-me dar . . .**
pod-meh dar . . .

a coat hanger?   **um cabide?**
oom cabeed

a towel?   **uma toalha?**
ooma too-al-ya

a glass?   **um copo?**
oom copoo

some soap?   **sabonete?**
saboonet

an ashtray?   **um cinzeiro?**
oom seenzayroo

another pillow?   **outra almofada?**
awtra almoofah-da

another blanket?   **outro cobertor?**
awtroo coobertor

Come in!   **Entre!**
entr

One moment, please!   **Um momento, por favor!**
oom moomentoo poor favor

Please can you . . .   **Por favor, pode . . .**
poor favor pod . . .

do this laundry/dry-
cleaning?   **lavar esta roupa/limpar a seco?**
lavar eh-shta rawpa/limp-ar ah
secoo

call me at . . .?   **me acordar às . . .**
meh acoordar ash . . .

help me with my luggage?   **me ajudar a carregar esta
bagagem?**
meh ajoodar a carregar eh-shta
bagajaim

call me a taxi for . . .?   **me chamar um taxi para . . .?**
[*For times, see p. 128*]   meh shamar oom taxi para . . .

The bill, please   **A conta, por favor**
a conta poor favor

Is service included?   **O serviço está incluído?**
oo serveessoo shtah eencloo-eedoo

I think this is wrong   **Acho que isto está errado**
ashoo ker eeshtoo shtah errah-doo

Can you give me a receipt?   **Pode-me dar um recibo?**
pod-meh dar oom reseeboo

At breakfast

Some more . . . please	**Mais . . . por favor** m*a*h-eesh . . . poor fav*o*r
coffee	**café** caf*e*h
tea	**chá** shah
bread	**pão** pown
butter	**manteiga** mant*ay*-ga
jam	**doce** d*o*ss
May I have a boiled egg?	**Queria um ovo quente** ker*ee*-a oom *a*wvoo k*e*nt

LIKELY REACTIONS

Have you an identity document, please?	**Tem algum documento de identificação, por favor?** taim alg*oo*m doocoomentoo der eedentee-feecass*a*wn poor fav*o*r
What's your name? *[see p. 16]*	**Como se chama?** c*o*moo ser sh*a*h-ma
Sorry, we're full	**Desculpe, estamos cheios** deshc*oo*lp shtamoosh sh*ay*-oosh
I haven't any rooms left	**Não tenho mais quartos** nown t*a*in-yoo m*a*h-eesh kw*a*rtoosh
Do you want to have a look?	**Quer ver?** k*ai*r vair
How many people is it for?	**Para quantas pessoas?** p*a*ra kw*a*ntash ps*a*w-ash
From (7 o'clock) onwards	**A partir das (sete) horas** a part*ee*r dash (set) *o*rash
From (midday) onwards *[For times, see p. 128]*	**A partir do (meio-dia)** a part*ee*r doo (m*a*y-oo d*ee*-a)
It's (63) escudos	**São (sessenta e três) escudos** sown (sess*e*nta ee tresh) shk*oo*doosh
[For numbers, see p. 126]	

Camping and youth hostelling

ESSENTIAL INFORMATION

Camping

● Look for the word: **CAMPING** or this sign

● Be prepared to have to pay:
per person
for the car (if applicable)
for the tent or caravan plot
for electricity
for hot showers
● You must provide proof of identity, such as your passport. In some parks it is necessary to show a camper's card or license, issued by a national or international organization that is officially recognized.
● Municipal-run sites are recommended.
● There are a number of limitations regarding camping off-site — check with the appropriate tourist office before departure.
● There are also a series of campsites with the **ORBITUR** sign — these provide bath, camping and bungalow facilities.
● Most of Portugal's campsites are situated along the coast — those inland are few and far between.

Youth hostels

- Look for the sign:
  POUSADA DE JUVENTUDE
- You must provide your own
  sleeping bag.
- You must have a YHA card.
- The charge for the night is
  the same for all ages, but
  some hostels are dearer
  than others.
- There are very few youth
  hostels in Portugal, and those
  that do exist provide
  dormitory accommodation. Few provide accommodation for girls.
  Cooking facilities are limited.
- Finding a campsite and a youth hostel, see p. 20.
- Replacing equipment, see p. 54.

WHAT TO SAY

I have a booking	**Tenho uma reserva** ta*in*-yoo *oo*ma reza*ir*va
Have you any vacancies?	**Tem espaço?** taim shp*a*ssoo
It's for . . .	**É para . . .** eh p*a*ra . . .
one adult/one person	**um adulto/uma pessoa** oom ad*oo*ltoo/*oo*ma ps*aw*-a
two adults/two people	**dois adultos/duas pessoas** doysh ad*oo*ltoosh/d*oo*-ash ps*aw*-ash
and one child	**e uma criança** ee *oo*ma cree-*a*nssa
and two children	**e duas crianças** ee d*oo*-ash cree-*a*nssash
It's for . . .	**É para . . .** eh p*a*ra . . .
one night	**uma noite** *oo*ma noyt
two nights	**duas noites** doo-ash noytsh
one week/two weeks	**uma semana/duas semanas** *oo*ma sem*a*h-na/d*oo*-ash sem*a*h-nash

How much is it . . .	**Quanto custa . . .** kwantoo cooshta . . .
for the tent?	**pela tenda?** pla tenda
for the caravan?	**pela roulotte?** pla roolot
for the car?	**pelo carro?** ploo carroo
for the electricity?	**pela electricidade?** pla eletreeseedad
per person?	**por pessoa?** poor psaw-a
per day/night?	**por dia/noite?** poor dee-a/noyt
May I look round?	**Posso ver?** possoo vair
Do you close the gate at night?	**Fecham o portão à noite?** fayshown oo poortown ah noyt
Do you provide anything . . .	**Fornecem alguma coisa . . .** foornessaim algooma coyza . . .
to eat?	**para comer?** para coomair
to drink?	**para beber?** para bebair
Do you have . . .	**Têm . . .** tay-aim . . .
a bar?	**um bar?** oom bar
hot showers?	**duches quentes?** dooshesh kentsh
a kitchen?	**uma cozinha?** ooma coozeen-ya
a laundry?	**uma lavandaria?** ooma lavandaree-a
a restaurant?	**um restaurante?** oom reshtah-oorant
a shop?	**uma loja?** ooma loja
a swimming pool?	**uma piscina?** ooma peesh-seena
a takeaway?	**comida preparada?** coomeeda preparahda

[*For food shopping, see p. 61, and for eating and drinking out, see p. 80*]

Where are . . .	**Onde são . . .**
	awnd sown . . .
the dustbins?	**os caixotes do lixo?**
	oosh ca-eeshotsh doo leeshoo
the showers?	**os duches?**
	oosh dooshesh
the toilets?	**as retretes?**
	ash retretsh
At what time must one . . .	**A que horas temos que . . .**
	a ker orash temoosh ker . . .
go to bed?	**deitar?**
	daytar
get up	**levantar?**
	levantar
Please, have you got . . .	**Por favor, têm . . .**
	poor favor tay-aim . . .
a broom?	**uma vassoura?**
	ooma vassaw-ra
a corkscrew?	**um saca rolhas?**
	oom sac-a rawl-yash
a drying-up cloth?	**um pano da loiça?**
	oom panoo dar loyssa
a fork?	**um garfo?**
	oom garfoo
a fridge?	**um frigorífico?**
	oom freegooreefeecoo
a frying pan?	**uma frigideira?**
	ooma freejeedayra
an iron?	**um ferro de engomar?**
	oom ferroo der engoomar
a knife?	**uma faca?**
	ooma fac-a
a plate?	**um prato?**
	oom prat-oo
a saucepan?	**um tacho?**
	oom tashoo
a teaspoon?	**uma colher de chá?**
	ooma kool-yair der shah
a tin-opener?	**um abre latas?**
	oom abrehlat-ash
any washing powder?	**detergente?**
	deterjent
any washing-up liquid?	**líquido para lavar a loiça?**
	leekeedoo para lavar ah loyssa

The bill, please	**A conta, por favor**
	a conta poor favor

Problems

The toilet	**A retrete**
	a retret
The shower	**O duche**
	oo doosh
The tap	**A torneira**
	a toornayra
The razor point	**A ficha de barbear**
	a feesha der barbee-ar
The light	**A luz**
	a loosh
. . . is not working	**. . . não funciona**
	. . . nown foonsee-awna
My camping gas has run out	**O gaz do meu fogão gastou-se**
	oo gash doo meh-oo foogown gashtaw-ser

LIKELY REACTIONS

Have you an identity document?	**Tem um documento de identificação?**
	taim oom doocoomentoo der eedenteefeeca-sown
Your membership card, please	**O seu cartão de membro, por favor**
	oo seh-oo cartown der mehm-broo poor favor
What's your name? [see p. 16]	**Como se chama?**
	comoo ser shah-ma
Sorry, we're full	**Desculpe, estamos cheios**
	deshcoolp shtamoosh shay-oosh
How many people is it for?	**Para quantas pessoas é?**
	para kwantash psaw-ash eh
How many nights is it for?	**Para quantas noites é?**
	para kwantash noytsh eh
It's (50) escudos . . .	**São (cinquenta) escudos . . .**
	sown (seenkwenta) shkoodoosh . . .
per day/per night [For numbers, see p. 126]	**por dia/por noite**
	poor dee-a/poor noyt

Rented accommodation: problem solving

ESSENTIAL INFORMATION

● If you're looking for accommodation to rent, look out for:
  PARA ALUGAR or **ALUGA-SE** (to let)
  APARTAMENTOS (small apartments)
  ANDARES (apartments)
  MORADIA (house with garden)
  VILLA (villa)
  CASA DE CAMPO (country house)
  QUINTA (farmhouse)
● For arranging details of your let, see 'Hotel', p. 27.
● Key words you will meet if renting on the spot:
  depósito   (deposit)
  dep*o*seetoo
  chave   (key)
  sh*a*hv
● Having arranged your own accommodation and arrived with the key, check the obvious basics that you take for granted at home.
  Electricity: Voltage? Razors and small appliances brought from home may need adjusting, as you will only find two pin plugs in Portugal.
  Gas: Town gas or bottled gas? Butane gas must be kept indoors, propane gas must be kept outdoors.
  Stove: Don't be surprised to find:
  —the grill inside the oven, or no grill at all.
  —a lid covering the rings which lifts up to form a 'splash-back'.
  —a mixture of two gas rings and two electric rings.
  Toilet: Mains drainage or septic tank? Don't flush disposable diapers or anything else down the toilet if you are on a septic tank.
  Water: Find the stopcock. Check taps and plugs—they may not operate in the way you are used to. Check how to turn on (or light) the hot water.
  Windows: Check the method of opening and closing windows and shutters.
  Insects: Is an insecticide provided? If not, get one locally.
  Equipment: For buying or replacing equipment, see p. 54.
● You will probably have an official agent, but be clear in your own mind who to contact in an emergency, even if it is only a neighbour in the first instance.

WHAT TO SAY

My name is . . .	**O meu nome é . . .** oo meh-oo nowm eh . . .
I'm staying at . . .	**Estou em . . .** shtaw aim . . .
They've cut off . . .	**Cortaram . . .** coortarown . . .
the electricity	**a electricidade** a eeletreesseedad
the gas	**o gaz** oo gash
the water	**a água** a ah-gwa
Is there . . . in the area?	**Existe na zona . . .** eezeesht na zawna . . .
an electrician	**um electricista?** oom eeletreesseeshta
a plumber	**um canalizador?** oom canaleezador
a gas fitter	**um canalizador de gaz?** oom canaleezador der gash
Where is . . .	**Onde é . . .** awnd eh . . .
the fuse box?	**o contador?** oo contador
the stopcock?	**a torneira principal?** a toornayra preenseepal
the boiler?	**a caldeira?** a caldayra
the water heater?	**o esquentador?** oo esh-kentador
Is there . . .	**Tem . . .** taim . . .
town gas?	**gaz central?** gash sentral
bottled gas?	**gaz de bilha?** gash der beel-ya
mains drainage?	**esgotos?** ej-gawtoosh

a septic tank?	**fossa séptica?** fossa set-eeca
central heating?	**aquecimento central?** akeh-seementoo sentral
The cooker	**O fogão** oo foogown
The hairdryer	**O secador** oo secador
The heating	**O aquecimento** oo akeh-seementoo
The immersion heater	**O esquentador** oo esh-kentador
The iron	**O ferro de engomar** oo ferroo der engoomar
The pilot light	**A chama piloto** a shah-ma peelawtoo
The refrigerator	**O frigorífico** oo freegooreeficoo
The telephone	**O telefone** oo telefon
The toilet	**A retrete** a retret
The washing machine	**A máquina de lavar** a makeena der lavar
. . . is not working	**. . . não funciona** . . . nown foonsee-awna
Where can I get . . .	**Onde posso obter . . .** awnd possoo obtair . . .
an adaptor for this?	**um adaptador para isto?** oom adaptador para eesh-too
a bottle of butane gas?	**uma bilha de gaz butano?** ooma beel-ya der gash bootanoo
a bottle of propane gas?	**uma bilha de gaz propano?** ooma beel-ya der gash proopanoo
a fuse?	**um fusível?** oom foozeevel
an insecticide spray?	**um atomizador de insecticida?** oom atoom-eezador der eenseteeseeda
a light bulb?	**uma lâmpada?** ooma lampada

The drain	**O esgoto**
	oo ej-gawtoo
The sink	**O lava-loiça**
	oo lava-loyssa
. . . is blocked	**. . . está entupido**
	. . . shtah entoopeedoo
The toilet is blocked	**A retrete está entupida**
	a retret shtah entoopeeda
The gas is leaking	**Há uma fuga de gaz**
	ah ooma fooga der gash
Can you mend it straightaway?	**Pode repar.-lo imediatamente?**
	pod reparah-loo eemedee-ahtament
When can you mend it?	**Quando é que o pode reparar?**
	kwandoo eh ker oo pod reparar
How much do I owe you?	**Quanto lhe devo?**
	kwantoo l-yeh devoo
When is the rubbish collected?	**Quando recolhem o lixo?**
	kwandoo recol-yem oo leeshoo

LIKELY REACTIONS

What's your name?	**Como se chama?**
	comoo ser shah-ma
What's your address?	**Qual é a sua morada?**
	kwal eh a soo-a moorah-da
There's a shop . . .	**Há uma loja . . .**
	ah ooma lo-sha . . .
in town	**na cidade**
	na seedad
in the village	**na aldeia**
	na alday-a
I can't come . . .	**Não posso vir . . .**
	nown possoo veer . . .
today	**hoje**
	awj
this week	**esta semana**
	eh-shta semah-na
until Monday	**até segunda-feira**
	ateh segoonda fayra

I can come ..	**Posso vir . . .** *possoo veer . . .*
on Tuesday	**na terça-feira** *na tairsa fayra*
when you want	**quando quiser** *kwandoo keezair*
Every day	**Todos os dias** *tawdoosh oosh dee-ash*
Every other day	**Dia sim, dia não** *dee-a seem dee-a nown*
On Wednesdays	**Às quartas-feiras** *ash kwartash fayrash*

[*For days of the week, see p. 130*]

General shopping

The drug store/The chemist's

ESSENTIAL INFORMATION

- Look for the word **FARMÁCIA** (drug store) or these signs: a cross or an 'H'.
- Medicines (drugs) are only available at a drug store.
- Some non-drugs can be bought at a supermarket or department store.
- Normal opening times are 9.00 a.m. to 1.00 p.m. and 3..00 p.m. to 7.00 p.m. From January to November, shops close at 1.00 p.m. on Saturday.
- If the drug store is shut the address of a nearby drug store on duty should be pinned on the door; if not, ask for the nearest **PRIMEIROS SOCORROS** (first aid centre). There may be an extra charge if after midnight (approx. 20%).
- Try the drug store before going to the doctor's as they are usually qualified to treat minor ailments.
- If you don't have insurance you'll have to pay the full rate. Keep receipts and packaging for the insurance claims.
- Some toiletries can also be bought at a **DROGARIA**.
- Finding a drug store, see p. 20.

WHAT TO SAY

I'd like . . . please	**Queria . . . por favor** ker*ee*-a . . . poor fav*o*r
some Alka Seltzer	**Alka Seltzer** alka seltzer
some antiseptic	**antiséptico** antees*e*ticoo
some aspirin	**aspirinas** aspeer*ee*nash
some bandage	**ligaduras** leegad*oo*rash
some cotton wool	**algodão** algood*ow*n
some eye drops	**pingos para os olhos** p*ee*ngoosh p*a*ra oosh *o*l-yoosh
some nose drops	**pingos para o nariz** p*ee*ngoosh p*a*ra oo nar*ee*sh
some foot powder	**pó para os pés** p*o* p*a*ra oosh p*e*sh
some gauze dressing	**gazes** g*ah*-zesh
some inhalant	**inalador** eenalad*o*r
some insect repellent	**repelente de insectos** repel*e*nt der eens*e*toosh
some lip salve	**creme para os lábios** cr*e*m p*a*ra oosh l*a*bee-oosh
some sticking plaster	**adesivo** ad-es*ee*voo
some throat pastilles	**pastilhas para a garganta** pasht*ee*l-yash p*a*ra ah garg*a*nta
some Vaseline	**Vaselina** vazel*ee*na
I'd like something for . . .	**Queria alguma coisa para . . .** ker*ee*-a alg*oo*ma c*o*yza p*a*ra . . .
bites/stings	**mordidelas** moordeed*e*l-ash
burns/scalds	**queimaduras** cay-mad*oo*rash
chilblains	**frieiras** free-*a*yrash

I'd like something for . . .	**Queria alguma coisa para . . .**
	keree-a algooma coyza para . . .
a cold	**constipação**
	consh-teepassown
constipation	**prisão de ventre**
	preezown der ventr
a cough	**tosse**
	toss
diarrhoea	**diarreia**
	dee-array-a
earache	**dor de ouvidos**
	dor der awveedoosh
flu	**gripe**
	greep
sore gums	**gengivas doridas**
	janjeevash dooreedash
sprains	**entorses**
	entohrsesh
sunburn	**queimadura do sol**
	cay-madoora doo sol
toothache	**dor de dentes**
	dor der dentsh
travel sickness	**enjoo de viagem**
	enjaw-oo der vee-ajaim
I need . . .	**Preciso de . . .**
	presseezo der . . .
some baby food	**comida para bébé**
	coomeeda para beh-beh
some contraceptives	**contraceptivos**
	contrasepteevoosh
some deodorant	**desodorizante**
	dezoh-dooreezant
some disposable nappies	**fraldas de papel**
	fral-dash der papel
some handcream	**creme para as mãos**
	crem para ash mowns
some lipstick	**baton**
	batawn
some make-up remover	**creme de limpeza**
	crem der leempeza
some paper tissues	**lenços de papel**
	lensoosh der papel

some razor blades	**lâminas para barbear**
	lameenash para barbee-ar
some safety pins	**alfinetes de ama**
	alfeenetsh der ah-ma
some sanitary towels	**pensos higiénicos**
	penssoosh eegee-en-eecoosh
some shaving cream	**creme de barbear**
	crem der barbee-ar
some soap	**sabonete**
	saboonet
some suntan lotion/oil	**loção/óleo para bronzear**
	lossown/olee-oo para brawnzee-ar
some talcum powder	**pó de talco**
	po der talcoo
some Tampax	**Tampax**
	tampax
some toilet paper	**papel higiénico**
	papel eegee-en-eecoo
some toothpaste	**pasta de dentes**
	pashta der dentsh

[*For other essential expressions, see 'Shop talk', p. 56*].

Holiday items

ESSENTIAL INFORMATION

● Places to shop at and signs to look for:
  PAPELARIA-LIVRARIA (stationery-bookshop)
  FOTOGRAFIA (films)
  and of course the main department stores:
  GRANDELLA
  ARMAZÉNS DO CHIADO

WHAT TO SAY

Where can I buy . . . ?	**Onde posso comprar . . . ?**
	awnd p*o*ssoo cawmpr*a*r . . .
I'd like . . .	**Queria . . .**
	ker*ee*-a . . .
a bag	**um saco**
	oom s*a*c-oo
a beach ball	**uma bola de praia**
	*oo*ma bol-a der pr*a*h-ya
a bucket	**um balde**
	oom b*a*hld
an English newspaper	**um jornal inglês**
	oom joorn*a*l eengl*e*sh
some envelopes	**envelopes**
	ainvel*o*psh
a guide book	**um guia**
	oom gu*ee*-a
a map (of the area)	**um mapa (da área)**
	oom m*a*h-pa (da *a*h-ree-a)
some postcards	**postais**
	poosht*a*h-eesh
a spade	**uma pá**
	*oo*ma p*a*h
a straw hat	**um chapéu de palha**
	oom shapeh-oo der p*a*l-ya
a suitcase	**uma mala**
	*oo*ma m*a*h-la
some sunglasses	**óculos de sol**
	*o*cooloosh der s*o*l

a sunshade	**um chapéu de sol**
	oom shapeh-oo der sol
an umbrella	**um chapéu de chuva**
	oom shapeh-oo der shoova
some writing paper	**papel de escrever**
	papel der shkrevair
I'd like . . . [*show the camera*]	**Queria . . .**
	keree-a . . .
a colour film	**um filme a côres**
	oom feelm ah cawresh
a black and white film	**um filme a preto e branco**
	oom feelm a pret-oo ee brancoo
for prints	**para fotografias**
	para footoografeeash
for slides	**para diapositivos**
	para dee-apoozeeteevoosh
12 (24/36) exposures	**de doze (vinte e quatro/trinta e seis) fotografias**
	der dawz (veent ee kwatroo/treenta ee saysh) footoografee-ash
a standard 8 mm film	**um film de oito milímetros normal**
	oom feelm der oytoo meeleemtroosh normal
a super 8 film	**um filme de super oito**
	oom feelm der sooper oytoo
some flash bulbs	**lâmpadas de flash**
	lampadash der flash
This camera is broken	**Esta máquina está partida**
	eh-shta makeena shtah parteeda
The film is stuck	**O filme está preso**
	oo feelm shtah prez-oo
Please can you . . .	**Pode . . .**
	pod . . .
develop/print this?	**revelar/imprimir isto?**
	revelar/eempreemeer eeshtoo
load the camera?	**carregar a máquina?**
	carregar a makeena

[*For other essential expressions, see 'Shop talk', p. 56*]

The smoke shop

ESSENTIAL INFORMATION

- A smoke shop is called a **TABACARIA.**
- To ask if there is one nearby, see p. 20.
- Smoke shops sometimes sell postage stamps.
- A smoke shop can be a part of a café: **CAFÉ-TABACARIA** or a stationery store: **PAPELARIA.**
- It is difficult to find both rolling and pipe tobacco in Portugal, so if you smoke either of these, take your own supply with you.

WHAT TO SAY

A packet of cigarettes . . .	**Um maço de cigarros . . .** oom massoo der seegarroosh . . .
with filters	**com filtro** com feeltroo
without filters	**sem filtro** saym feeltroo
king size	**gigante** jeegant
menthol	**de mentol** der mentol
Those up there . . .	**Aqueles ali . . .** akel-esh alee . . .
on the right	**à direita** ah deerayta
on the left	**à esquerda** ah shkairda
These [point]	**Estes** eshtesh
Cigarettes, please . . .	**Cigarros, por favor . . .** seegarroosh poor favor . . .
100, 200, 300	**Cem, duzentos, trezentos** saim, doozentoosh, trez-entoosh
Two packets	**Dois maços** doysh massoos

Do you have . . .	**Tem . . .** taim . . .
English cigarettes?	**cigarros ingleses?** seegarroosh eenglezesh
American cigarettes?	**cigarros americanos?** seegarroosh americanoosh
English pipe tobacco?	**tabaco de cachimbo inglês?** tabacoo der casheemboo eenglesh
American pipe tobacco?	**tabaco de cachimbo americano?** tabacoo der casheemboo americanoo
rolling tobacco?	**tabaco avulso?** tabacoo avoolsoo
A packet of pipe tobacco	**Um pacote de tabaco de cachimbo** oom pacot der tabacoo der casheemboo
That one up there . . .	**Aquele ali . . .** akel alee . . .
on the right	**à direita** ah deerayta
on the left	**à esquerda** ah shkairda
That one [*point*]	**Aquele** akel
A cigar, please	**Um charuto, por favor** oom sharootoo poor favor
This one [*point*]	**Este** esht
Some cigars, please	**Charutos, por favor** sharootoosh poor favor
Those [*point*]	**Aqueles** akel-esh
A box of matches	**Uma caixa de fósforos** ooma cah-eesha der fosh-froosh
A packet of flints [*show lighter*]	**Um pacote de pedras de isqueiro** oom pacot der pedrash der eesh-cayroo
Lighter fuel	**Gasolina para isqueiro** gazooleena para eesh-cayroo
Lighter gas, please	**Gaz para isqueiro, por favor** gash para eesh-cayroo poor favor

[*For other essential expressions, see 'Shop talk', p. 56*]

Buying clothes

ESSENTIAL INFORMATION

- Look for:
  ROUPA DE SENHORA (women's clothes)
  ROUPA DE HOMEM (men's clothes)
  ROUPA DE CRIANÇA (children's clothes)
  SAPATARIA (shoe shop)
- Don't buy without being measured first or without trying things on.
- Don't rely on conversion charts of clothing sizes (see p. 141).
- If you are buying for someone else, take their measurements with you.

WHAT TO SAY

I'd like . . .	**Queria . . .**
	keree-a . . .
an anorak	**um anoraque**
	oom anorak
a belt	**um cinto**
	oom seentoo
a bikini	**um bikini**
	oom bikini
a bra	**um soutien**
	oom sootee-an
a cap (swimming)	**uma touca (de banho)**
	ooma tawka (der bain-yoo)
a cap (skiing)	**um gorro (de ski)**
	oom gawrroo (der ski)
a cardigan	**um casaco de malha**
	oom cazac-oo der mal-ya
a coat	**um casaco comprido**
	oom cazac-oo coompreed-oo
a dress	**um vestido**
	oom veshteedoo
a hat	**um chapéu**
	oom shapeh-oo
a jacket	**um casaco**
	oom cazac-oo

a jumper	**uma camisola**
	*oo*ma cameezol-a
a nightdress	**uma camisa de dormir**
	*oo*ma cam*ee*za der doorm*ee*r
a pullover	**um pulover**
	oom pul*o*ver
a raincoat	**uma gabardina**
	*oo*ma gabard*ee*na
a shirt	**uma camisa**
	*oo*ma cam*ee*za
a skirt	**uma saia**
	*oo*ma s*a*h-ee-a
a suit	**um fato**
	oom f*a*h-too
a swimsuit	**um fato de banho**
	oom f*a*h-too der b*a*in-yoo
a tee-shirt	**um teeshirt**
	oom teeshirt
I'd like a pair of . . .	**Queria . . .**
	ker*ee*-a . . .
shorts	**uns shortes**
	oomsh shortsh
stockings	**umas meias**
	*oo*mash m*a*y-ash
tights	**meias calças**
	m*a*y-ash c*a*lsash
pyjamas	**um pijama**
	oom peej*a*ma
I'd like a pair of . . .	**Queria um par de . . .**
	ker*ee*-a oom par der . . .
briefs (men and women)	**cuecas**
	coo-*eh*-cash
gloves	**luvas**
	l*oo*vash
jeans	**jeans**
	jeans
socks	**peúgas**
	p*e*wgash
trousers	**calças**
	c*a*lsash

I'd like a pair of . . .	**Queria um par de . . .** ker*ee*-a oom par der . . .
shoes	**sapatos** sap*a*t-oosh
canvas shoes	**sapatos de pano** sap*a*t-oosh der pan*oo*
sandals	**sandálias** sand*a*l-ee-ash
beach shoes	**sapatos de praia** sap*a*t-oosh der pr*ah*-ya
smart shoes	**sapatos elegantes** sap*a*t-oosh eeleg*a*ntsh
boots	**botas** b*o*t-ash
moccasins	**mocasines** moc-as*ee*nsh
My size is . . .	**O meu número é . . .** oo meh-oo n*oo*meroo eh . . .

[*For numbers, see p. 126*]

Can you measure me, please?	**Pode tirar-me a medida, por favor?** pod t*ee*rar-meh ah med*ee*da poor favor
Can I try it on?	**Posso prová-lo?** p*o*ssoo proov*ah*-loo
It's for a present	**É para dar** eh p*a*ra d*a*r
These are the measurements . . . [*show written*]	**Estas são as medidas . . .** *e*shtash sown ash med*ee*dash . . .
bust	**peito** p*a*ytoo
chest	**peito** p*a*ytoo
collar	**colarinho** coolar*ee*n-yoo
hips	**ancas** *a*ncash
leg	**perna** p*a*irna
waist	**cintura** seent*oo*ra

Have you got something . . .	**Tem alguma coisa . . .**
	taim algooma coyza . . .
in black?	**em preto?**
	aim pretoo
in white?	**em branco?**
	aim brancoo
in grey?	**em cinzento?**
	aim seenzentoo
in blue?	**em azul?**
	aim azool
in brown?	**em castanho?**
	aim cashtan-yoo
in pink?	**em cor de rosa?**
	aim cor der roza
in green?	**em verde?**
	aim vaird
in red?	**em vermelho?**
	aim vermayl-yoo
in yellow?	**em amarelo?**
	aim amarel-oo
in this colour [*point*]	**nesta cor?**
	neshta cor
in cotton?	**de algodão?**
	der algoodown
in denim?	**de ganga?**
	der ganga
in leather?	**de cabedal?**
	der cab-ed-al
in nylon?	**de nylon?**
	der nah-eelon
in suede?	**de camurça?**
	der camoorsa
in wool?	**de lã?**
	der lan
in this material? [*point*]	**deste tecido?**
	desht tesseedoo

[*For other essential expressions, see 'Shop talk', p. 56*]

Replacing equipment

ESSENTIAL INFORMATION

- Look for these shops and signs:
  LOJA DE FERRAGENS (hardware)
  ELECTRO-DOMÉSTICOS (electrical goods)
  DROGARIA (household cleaning materials)
- In a supermarket, look for this display: **FERRAGENS.**
- To ask the way to the shop, see p. 20.
- At a campsite try their shop first.

WHAT TO SAY

Have you got . . .	**Tem . . .**
	taim . . .
an adaptor?	**uma ficha adaptadora?**
[*show appliance*]	*oo*ma f*ee*sha adaptad*o*ra
a bottle of butane gas?	**uma bilha de gaz butano?**
	*oo*ma b*ee*l-ya der gash boot*a*noo
a bottle of propane gas?	**uma bilha de gaz propano?**
	*oo*ma b*ee*l-ya der gash proop*a*noo
a bottle opener?	**um abre garrafas?**
	oom *a*br garr*a*fash
a corkscrew?	**um saca rolhas?**
	oom s*a*c-a r*a*wl-yash
any disinfectant?	**desinfectante?**
	dezeen-fet*a*nt
any disposable cups?	**copos de papel?**
	c*o*poosh der pap*e*l
any disposable plates?	**pratos de papel?**
	pr*a*t-oosh der pap*e*l
a drying-up cloth?	**um pano da loiça?**
	oom p*a*noo da l*o*yssa
any forks?	**garfos?**
	g*a*rfoosh
a fuse? [*show old one*]	**um fusível?**
	oom fooz*ee*vel
an insecticide spray?	**um atomizador de insecticida?**
	oom atoomeezad*o*r der ensetees*ee*da

a paper kitchen roll?	**um rolo de cozinha de papel?**
	oom *r*awloo der coozeen-ya der papel
any knives?	**facas?**
	*f*acash
a light bulb? [*show old one*]	**uma lâmpada?**
	*oo*ma lampada
a plastic bucket?	**um balde de plástico?**
	oom b*a*hld der plashticoo
a plastic can?	**uma lata de plástico?**
	*oo*ma lah-ta der plashticoo
a scouring pad?	**um esfregão?**
	oom shfreg*o*wn
a spanner?	**uma chave de porcas?**
	*oo*ma shahv der porcash
a sponge?	**uma esponja?**
	*oo*ma shp*a*wnja
any string?	**cordel?**
	coord*e*l
any tent pegs?	**pregos de tenda?**
	preg*o*osh der tenda
a tin opener?	**um abre latas?**
	oom abr l*a*t-ash
a torch?	**uma lanterna?**
	*oo*ma lant*a*irna
any torch batteries	**pilhas para lanterna?**
	p*ee*l-yash para lant*a*irna
a universal plug (for the sink)?	**uma válvula universal (para o lava-loiças)?**
	*oo*ma valvoola ooneevers*a*l (para oolav*a*-l*o*yssash)
a washing line?	**uma corda da roupa?**
	*oo*ma corda da r*a*wpa
any washing powder?	**detergente?**
	deterg*e*nt
any washing-up liquid?	**líquido de lavar a loiça?**
	l*ee*keedoo der lav*a*r a loyssa
a washing-up brush?	**uma escova de lavar a loiça?**
	*oo*ma shk*a*wva der lav*a*r a l*o*yssa

[*For other essential expressions, see 'Shop talk', p. 56*]

Shop talk

ESSENTIAL INFORMATION

- Know your coins and bills:
  coins: see illustration. The 10$00 coin is not widely in circulation.
  bills: 20, 50, 100, 500 and 1000 escudos.
- Know how to say the important weights and measures:

50 grams	**cinquenta gramas**
	seenkwenta gram-ash
100 grams	**cem gramas**
	saim gram-ash
200 grams	**duzentas gramas**
	doozent-ash gram-ash
½ kilo	**meio quilo**
	may-oo keeloo
1 kilo	**um quilo**
	oom keeloo
2 kilos	**dois quilos**
	doysh keeloosh
½ litre	**meio litro**
	may-oo leetroo
1 litre	**um litro**
	oom leetroo
2 litres	**dois litros**
[*For numbers, see p. 126*]	doysh leetroosh

- In small shops don't be surprised if customers, as well as the shop
  assistant, say 'hello' and 'goodbye' to you.

CUSTOMER

Hello	**Olá** ol*ah*
Good morning	**Bom dia** bom d*ee*-a
Good afternoon	**Boa tarde** b*oa* t*ar*d
Goodbye	**Adeus** ad*eh*-oosh
I'm just looking	**Estou só a ver** shtaw s*oh* a vair
Excuse me	**Com licença** com lees*en*-sa
How much is this/that?	**Quanto custa isto/aquilo?** kwantoo c*oo*shta *ee*shtoo/ak*ee*loo
What is that?	**O que é aquilo?** oo ker *eh* ak*ee*loo
What are those?	**O que são aqueles?** oo ker sown ak*el*-esh
Is there a discount?	**Faz desconto?** fash desh-c*aw*ntoo
I'd like that, please	**Queria aquilo, por favor** ker*ee*-a ak*ee*loo poor fav*o*r
Not that	**Esse não** *eh*sse nown
Like that	**Como aquele** c*o*moo ak*el*
That's enough, thank you	**Chega obrigado/a*** sh*eg*-a obreeg*ah*-doo/a
More, please	**Mais, por favor** m*ah*-eesh poor fav*o*r
Less	**Menos** m*en*-oosh
That's fine	**Está bem** shtah baim
OK	**OK** *o*h kay
I won't take it, thank you	**Não quero, obrigado/a*** nown k*e*roo obreeg*ah*-doo/a

*First alternative for men, second for women.

It's not right	**Não está certo**
	nown shtah s*ai*rtoo
Thank you very much	**Muito obrigado/a***
	moo-*ee*too obreeg*a*h-doo/a
Have you got something . . .	**Tem alguma coisa . . .**
	taim alg*oo*ma c*o*yza . . .
better?	**melhor?**
	mel-y*o*r
cheaper?	**mais barata?**
	m*a*h-eesh bar*a*ta
different?	**diferente?**
	deefer*e*nt
larger?	**maior?**
	ma-y*o*r
smaller?	**mais pequena?**
	m*a*h-eesh pek*e*na
At what time do you . . .	**A que horas . . .**
	a ker *o*rash . . .
open?	**abrem?**
	*a*braim
close?	**fecham?**
	f*a*yshown
Can I have a bag, please?	**Posso ter um saco, por favor?**
	p*o*sso tair oom s*a*c-oo poor fav*o*r
Can I have a receipt?	**Posso ter um recibo, por favor?**
	p*o*sso tair oom res*ee*boo poor fav*o*r
Do you take . . .	**Aceita . . .**
	as*a*yta . . .
English/American money?	**dinheiro inglês/americano?**
	deen-y*a*yroo eenglesh/americ*a*noo
travellers' cheques?	**cheques de viagem?**
	sh*e*h-ksh der vee-*a*jaim
credit cards?	**cartões de crédito?**
	cart*o*ynsh der cr*e*deetoo
I'd like . . .	**Queria . . .**
	ker*ee*-a . . .
one like that	**um assim**
	oom ass*ee*m
two like that	**dois assim**
	d*o*ysh ass*ee*m

*First alternative for men, second for women.

SHOP ASSISTANT

Can I help you?	**Deseja alguma coisa?**
	dezay-ja algooma coyza
What would you like?	**Que quer?**
	ker kair
Will that be all?	**Não é mais nada?**
	nown eh mah-eesh nah-da
Is that all?	**É tudo?**
	eh toodoo
Anything else?	**Mais alguma coisa?**
	mah-eesh algooma coyza
Would you like it wrapped?	**Quer embrulhado?**
	kair embrool-yah-doo
Sorry, none left	**Desculpe, está esgotado**
	deshcoolp shtah esh-gootah-doo
I haven't got any	**Não tenho**
	nown tain-yoo
I haven't got any more	**Não tenho mais**
	nown tain-yoo mah-eesh
How many do you want?	**Quantos quer?**
	kwantoosh kair
How much do you want?	**Quanto quer?**
	kwantoo kair
Is that enough?	**Chega?**
	sheg-a

Shopping for food

Bread

ESSENTIAL INFORMATION
- Finding a baker's, see p. 20; key words to look for:
  PADARIA (baker's) **PADEIRO** (baker) **PÃO** (bread)
- Supermarkets and general stores nearly always sell bread.
- Bakeries will open weekdays from 7.30 a.m. – 12.30 p.m. and from 5.30 p.m. – 8.00 p.m. They also open on Saturday mornings.
- The most characteristic bread is a small individual bread roll called **papo seco** which is sold by item.
- For any other type of loaf, say **um pão** (oom pown), and point.

WHAT TO SAY

Some bread, please	**Pão, por favor** pown poor fav*o*r
A loaf (like that)	**Um pão de forma (assim)** oom pown deh f*o*rma (ass*ee*m)
A home-made loaf	**Um pão caseiro** oom pown caz*ay*-roo
A French loaf	**Um cacete** oom cah-s*e*t
A large one	**Um grande** oom grand
A small one	**Um pequeno** oom pek*e*noo
A bread roll	**Um papo seco** oom p*a*p-oo s*e*c-oo
A crescent roll	**Um croissant** oom croo-*a*hssan
Two loaves	**Dois pães de forma** doysh p*a*-eensh der f*o*rma
Two home made loaves	**Dois pães caseiros** doysh p*a*-eensh caz*ay*-roosh
Four bread rolls	**Quatro papo secos** kw*a*troo p*a*p-oo s*e*c-oosh
A sliced loaf	**Um pão às fatias** oom pown ash fat*ee*-ash
A wholemeal loaf	**Um pão integral** oom pown eentegr*a*l

[*For other essential expressions, see 'Shop talk' p. 56*]

Cakes

ESSENTIAL INFORMATION

- Key words to look for:
  PASTELARIA (cake shop)
  CAFÉ (a place where cakes and sandwiches can be bought to be eaten on the premises or taken away – alcoholic drinks are also served)
  PADEIRO (baker – some also sell fresh cakes)
- To find a cake shop, see p. 20.
- **CASA DE CHÁ** (a tea shop usually open during the afternoon)
- Ordering a drink, see p. 80.

WHAT TO SAY

The types of cakes you find in shops varies from region to region but the following are the most common:

bola de Berlim	doughnut
bol-a der berleen	
duchesse	cream-filled choux pastry
dooshez	
pastel de nata	custard tart
pashtel der nah-ta	
bolo de côco	coconut tart
bawloo der cawcoo	
pão de ló	sponge
pown der loh	
queque	cupcake
kek	
palmier	flat, crispy pastry biscuit
palmee-eh	
mil folhas	crispy pastry with fresh cream filling
meel fawl-yash	– mille feuilles
suspiro	meringue (bought by weight)
soospeeroo	
tarte de amêndoa	almond tart
tart der amaindoo-a	
bolo de noz	walnut cake
bawloo der noj	

petits fours pet*ee* foor	petits fours (bought by weight)
queijadas de sintra cay-j*a*-dash der s*i*ntra	individual cheesecakes
fios de ovos f*ee*-oosh der *o*voosh **ovos moles** *o*voosh m*o*lesh	very sweet, egg-based confectionery

You usually buy medium-sized cakes by number:

Two doughnuts, please	**Duas bolas de Berlim, por favor** d*oo*-ash b*o*l-ash der berl*ee*n poor fav*o*r

Small cakes and biscuits by weight:

400 grams of petits fours	**Quatrocentas gramas de petits fours** kwatros*e*nt-ash gr*a*m-ash der pet*ee* foor

Large cakes by the slice:

One slice of almond tart	**Uma fatia de tarte de amêndoa** *oo*ma fat*ee*-a der tart der am*a*ind*oo*-a
Two slices of walnut cake	**Duas fatias de bolo de noz** d*oo*-ash fat*ee*-ash der b*a*wloo der noj

You may also want to say:

A selection, please	**Um sortido, por favor** oom soort*ee*doo poor fav*o*r

[*For other essential expressions, see 'Shop talk', p. 56*]

Ice-cream and sweets

ESSENTIAL INFORMATION

- Key words to look for:
  GELADOS (ice-cream)
  GELATARIA (ice-cream parlour)
  CONFEITARIA (sweet shop)
  PASTELARIA (cake shop)
- Best known ice-cream brands are:
  OLÁ and **RAJÁ**
- Ice-cream is sold by price (i.e. a ten-escudo cone).
- Prepacked sweets are available in general stores and supermarkets.

WHAT TO SAY

A . . . ice, please	**Um gelado . . . por favor** oom gelah-doo . . . poor favor
almond	**de amêndoa** der amaindoo-a
banana	**de banana** der banana
chocolate	**de chocolate** der shookoolat
strawberry	**de morango** der moorangoo
vanilla	**de baunilha** der bah-ooneel-ya
A (ten-escudo) cone	**Um cone de (dez escudos)** oom con der (desh shkoodoosh)
A (ten-escudo) tub	**Um copo de (dez escudos)** oom copoo der (desh shkoodoosh)
A mixed cone	**Um cone misto** oom con meeshtoo
A lollipop	**Um chupa-chupa** oom shoopa-shoopa
A packet of . . .	**Um pacote de . . .** oom pacot der . . .
chewing gum	**chewing gum** chewing gum

100 grams of . . .	**Cem gramas de . . .** saim gram-ash der . . .
200 grams of . . .	**Duzentas gramas de . . .** doozent-ash gram-ash der . . .
sweets	**rebuçados** reboossah-doosh
toffees	**caramelos** caramel-oosh
chocolates	**bonbons** bom-bomsh
mints	**rebuçados de mentol** reboossah-doosh der mentol
A bar of chocolate	**Uma tablete de chocolate** ooma ta-blet der shookoolat

[*For other essential expressions, see 'Shop talk', p. 56*]

In the supermarket

ESSENTIAL INFORMATION

- The place to ask for:
  UM SUPERMERCADO (supermarket)
- Key instructions on signs in the shop:
  ENTRADA (entrance)
  ENTRADA PROIBIDA (no entry)
  SAÍDA (exit)
  SAÍDA PROIBIDA (no exit)
  SEM SAÍDA (no way out)
  SAÍDA PARA NÃO COMPRADORES (exit for non-buyers)
  CAIXA (check-out, cash desk)
  MENOS DE 6 ARTIGOS (check-out for up to six items)
  OFERTA ESPECIAL (on offer)
  SELF-SERVICE (self-service)
- Supermarkets are open from 9.00 a.m. to 1.00 p.m. and 3.00 p.m. to 7.00 p.m. and Saturday mornings.
- No need to say anything in a supermarket, but ask if you can't see what you want.

WHAT TO SAY

Excuse me, please	**Com licença, por favor** com leesensa poor favor
Where is . . .	**Onde está . . .** awnd shtah . . .
the bread?	**o pão?** oo pown
the butter?	**a manteiga?** a mantay-ga
the cheese?	**o queijo?** oo cay-joo
the chocolate?	**o chocolate?** oo shookoolat
the coffee?	**o café?** oo cafeh
the cooking oil?	**o óleo?** oo ol-ee-oo

the fresh fish section?	**o peixe fresco?**
	oo paysh freshcoo
the frozen foods?	**a comida congelada?**
	a coomeeda conjelah-da
the fruit?	**a fruta?**
	a froota
the jam	**a compota?**
	a compot-a
the meat?	**a carne?**
	a carn
the milk?	**o leite?**
	oo late
the mineral water?	**a água mineral?**
	a ah-gwa meeneral
the salt?	**o sal?**
	oo sal
the sugar?	**o açúcar?**
	oo assoo-car
the tea?	**o chá?**
	oo shah
the tinned fish?	**o peixe em lata?**
	oo paysh aim lat-a
the tinned fruit?	**a fruta em lata?**
	a froota aim lat-a
the vinegar?	**o vinagre?**
	oo veenagr
the wine?	**o vinho?**
	oo veen-yoo
the yogurt?	**o iogurte?**
	oo yogoort
Where are . . .	**Onde estão . . .**
	awnd shtown . . .
the biscuits?	**as bolachas?**
	ash boolashash
the crisps?	**as batatas fritas?**
	ash batatash freetash
the eggs?	**os ovos?**
	oosh ovoosh
the fruit juices?	**os sumos de fruta?**
	oos soomoos der froota
the pastas?	**as massas?**
	ash massash

Where are . . .	**Onde estão . . .**
	awnd shtown . . .
the sausages?	**as salsichas?**
	ash salseeshash
the soft drinks?	**as bebidas não alcoólicas?**
	ash bebeedash nown alkoo-oleekash
the sweets?	**os rebuçados?**
	oosh reboossah-dosh
the tinned vegetables?	**os legumes em lata?**
	oosh legoomsh aim lat-a
the vegetables?	**os legumes?**
	oosh legoomsh

[*For other essential expressions, see 'Shop talk' p. 56*]

Picnic food

ESSENTIAL INFORMATION

- Key words to look for:
  CHARCUTARIA (pork butcher's, delicatessen)
  MERCEARIA (grocer's)
- Weight guide:
  4–6 oz/150 g of prepared salad per two people, if eaten as a starter
  to a substantial meal.
  3–4 oz/100 g of prepared salad per person, if to be eaten as the
  main part of a picnic-type meal.
- Cold meats bought by weight – slices are thin unless otherwise
  specified.

WHAT TO SAY

One slice of . . .	**Uma fatia de . . .** *oo*ma fat*ee*-a der . . .
Two slices of . . .	**Duas fatias de . . .** d*oo*-ash fat*ee*-ash der . . .
ham	**fiambre** fee-*a*mbr
roast pork	**carne de porco assada** carn der p*o*rcoo ass*a*h-da
spam	**mortadela** moortad*e*la
salami	**salame** sal*a*m
meaty garlic sausage	**paio** pah-*ee*-oo
(parma) ham	**presunto** prez*oo*ntoo
tongue	**língua** l*ee*ngwa
100 grams of . . .	**Cem gramas de . . .** saim gr*a*m-ash der . . .
150 grams of . . .	**Cento e cinquenta gramas de . . .** s*e*ntoo ee seenkw*e*nta gr*a*m-ash der . . .

200 grams of . . .	**Duzentas gramas de . . .**
	doozent-ash gram-ash der . . .
300 grams of . . .	**Trezentas gramas de . . .**
	trezent-ash gram-ash der . . .

Russian salad	**salada russa**
	salah-da roossa
tomato salad	**salada de tomate**
	salah-da der toomat
seafood salad	**salada de mariscos**
	salah-da der mareesh-coosh
olives (green/black)	**azeitonas (verdes/pretas)**
	azaytawnash (vairdesh/pretash)
anchovies	**anchovas**
	anshawvash
cheese	**queijo**
	cay-joo

You might also like to try some of these:

salada de feijão frade	black-eyed bean salad
salah-da der fay-jown frad	
croquetes	tiny meat rolls
croketsh	
pastéis de bacalhau	cod in batter
pashtaysh der bacal-yah-oo	
rissóis de camarão	shrimp rissoles
rissoysh der camarown	
chouriço	garlic sausage
shawreesso	
chouriço de carne	beefy garlic sausage
shawreessoo der carn	
pastéis de massa folhada/	meat/fish vol-au-vent
de carne/de peixe	
pashtaysh der massa fool-yah-da/der carn/der paysh	
panados de galinha	chicken pieces in breadcrumbs
panah-dosh der galeen-ya	
salsichas	sausages
salseeshash	
linguiça	very thin sausage
leengoo-eessa	
farinheira	floury pork sausage
fareen-yay-ra	

tremoços trem*oss*osh	lupin seeds (served with beer in cervejarias)
pevides pev*ee*dsh	dried and salted pumpkin seeds
castanhas assadas casht*an*-yash ass*ah*-dash	roast chestnuts
favas fritas f*a*vash fr*ee*tash	fried broad beans (served up as cocktail 'nibbles')
queijo fresco c*ay*-joo fr*e*shcoo	fresh goat's cheese (unsalted)
requeijão recay-j*o*wn	fresh sheep's cheese
queijo da serra c*ay*-joo da s*e*rra	tasty full-fat cheese
queijo das Ilhas c*ay*-joo dash *ee*l-yash	strong hard cheese (like Cheddar)
queijo de Serpa c*ay*-joo der s*ai*rpa	melting cheese (delicacy of the town of Serpa)
ovos cozidos *o*voosh cooz*ee*doosh	hard-boiled eggs
almôndegas alm*a*wndeegash	meatballs
empadas de galinha/marisco aimp*ah*-dash der gal*ee*n-ya/ mar*ee*sh-coo	chicken/shellfish pies
frango no churrasco fr*a*ngoo noo shoorr*a*sh-coo	chicken on the spit (spicy)
ovos verdes *o*voosh v*ai*rdesh	hard-boiled eggs with yolks mashed with parsley
arroz doce *a*rrawsh daws	sweet rice with lemon peel and cinnamon
pudim molotoff p*oo*dim molotof	egg-white pudding with caramel sauce
queijo de Évora c*ay*-joo der *e*voora	small, round, very hard, dried cheese

[*For other essential expressions, see 'Shop talk', p. 56*]

Fruit and vegetables

ESSENTIAL INFORMATION

- Key words to look for:
  FRUTA (fruit)
  FRUTARIA (greengrocer's)
  LEGUMES (vegetables)
  FRESCO (an indication of freshness)
- Weight guide:
  1 kilo of potatoes is sufficient for six people for one meal.
- If possible, buy fruit and vegetables in the market (**praça** or **mercado**) where they are cheaper and fresher than in the shops.

WHAT TO SAY

½ kilo (1 lb) of . . .	**Meio quilo de . . .**
	m*a*y-oo k*ee*loo der . . .
1 kilo of . . .	**Um quilo de . . .**
	oom k*ee*loo der . . .
2 kilos of . . .	**Dois quilos de . . .**
	doysh k*ee*loosh der . . .
apples	**maçãs**
	mas*a*nsh
apricots	**alperces**
	alp*ai*rssesh
bananas	**bananas**
	ban*a*nash
cherries	**cerejas**
	ser*a*y-jash
grapes (white/black)	**uvas (brancas/pretas)**
	*oo*vash (br*a*ncash/pr*e*tash)
greengages	**rainhas cláudias**
	ra-*ee*n-yash cl*ou*d-ee-ash
oranges	**laranjas**
	lar*a*njash
peaches	**pêssegos**
	p*e*h-segoosh
pears	**pêras**
	p*e*rash

plums	**ameixas** am*a*y-shash
strawberries	**morangos** moor*a*ngoosh
A pineapple, please	**Um ananás . . . por favor** oom anan*a*sh poor fav*o*r
A grapefruit	**Uma toranja** *oo*ma toor*a*nja
A melon	**Um melão** oom mel*o*wn
A water melon	**Uma melancia** *oo*ma melans*ee*-a
250 grams of . . .	**Duzentas e cinquenta gramas de . . .** doo*z*ent-ash ee seenkw*e*nta gram-ash der . . .
½ kilo of . . .	**Meio quilo de . . .** m*a*y-oo k*ee*loo der . . .
1 kilo of . . .	**Um quilo de . . .** oom k*ee*loo der . . .
1½ kilos of . . .	**Um quilo e meio de . . .** oom k*ee*loo ee m*a*y-oo der . . .
2 kilos of . . .	**Dois quilos de . . .** doysh k*ee*loosh der . . .
artichokes	**alcachofras** alkashoh-frash
broad beans	**favas** f*a*v-ash
carrots	**cenouras** sen*a*wrash
green beans	**feijão verde** fay-j*o*wn vaird
leeks	**alhos franceses** *a*l-yoosh franses-esh
mushrooms	**cogumelos** coogoom*e*l-oosh
onions	**cebolas** seb*a*wlash
peas	**ervilhas** airv*ee*l-yash
potatoes	**batatas** bat*a*tash

2 kilos of . . .	**Dois quilos de . . .**
	doysh keeloosh der . . .
shallots	**chalotas**
	shalo-tash
spinach	**espinafre**
	shpeenafr
tomatoes	**tomates**
	toomatsh
A bunch of . . .	**Um molho de . . .**
	oom mawl-yoo der . . .
parsley	**salsa**
	salsa
radishes	**rabanetes**
	rabanetsh
A head of garlic	**Uma cabeça de alho**
	ooma cabeh-sa der al-yoo
A lettuce	**Uma alface**
	ooma alfass
A cauliflower	**Uma couve flor**
	ooma cawv floor
A cabbage	**Uma couve**
	ooma cawv
A cucumber	**Um pepino**
	oom pepeenoo
A turnip	**Um nabo**
	oom naboo
Like that, please	**Assim, por favor**
	asseem poor favor

Fruit and vegetables which may not be familiar:

romãs	pomegranates
roomansh	
maracujá	passion fruit
marakoojah	
nêsperas	medlars: slightly sour fruit, orange
neshperash	in colour and juicy.
grelos	green cabbage sprouts
greh-loosh	
coentros	fresh coriander
kwentroosh	

Meat

ESSENTIAL INFORMATION

- Key word to look for:
  TALHO (butcher's)
- Weight guide: 4–6 oz/125–200 g of meat per person for one meal.
- The diagrams on p. 76 are to help you make sense of labels on counters and supermarket displays, and decide which cut or joint to have. Translations do not help, and you don't need to say the Portuguese word involved.

WHAT TO SAY

For a joint, choose the type of meat and then say
how many people it is for:

Some beef, please	**Carne de vaca, por favor** carn der vac-a poor favor
Some lamb	**Carne de cordeiro** carn der coorday-roo
Some mutton	**Carne de carneiro** carn der carnay-roo
Some pork	**Carne de porco** carn der porcoo
Some veal	**Carne de vitela** carn der veetel-a
A joint . . .	**Uma peça . . .** ooma pehsa . . .
for two people	**para duas pessoas** para doo-ash psaw-ash
for four people	**para quatro pessoas** para kwatroo psaw-ash
for six people	**para seis pessoas** para saysh psaw-ash

For steak, liver or kidneys, do as above:

Some steak, please	**Bifes, por favor** beefsh poor favor
Some liver	**Fígado** feegadoo

Beef Vaca

1 Cachaço
2 Pá e acém
3 Peito alto
4 Rosbife completo
5 Prego do peito
6 Alcatra
7 Perna

Veal Vitela

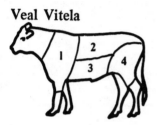

1 Pá
2 Randa das costelas
3 Peito
4 Perna

Pork Porco

1 Fim do pescoço
2 Mão
3 Lombada
4 Entrecosto
5 Barriga
6 Perna

Lamb Cordeiro

1 Pescoço
2 Carré
3 Espádua
4 Lombo
5 Vão de costelas ou peito
6 Perna

Some kidneys	**Rins** reensh
Some sausages	**Salsichas** salseeshash
for three people	**para três pessoas** para tresh psaw-ash
for five people	**para cinco pessoas** para seencoo psaw-ash

For chops do it this way:

Two veal escalopes, please	**Dois escalopes de vitela, por favor** doysh shcalopsh der veetel-a poor favor
Three pork chops	**Três costoletas de porco** tresh cooshtoolet-ash der porcoo
Four mutton chops	**Quatro costoletas de carneiro** kwatroo cooshtoolet-ash der carnay-roo
Five lamb chops	**Cinco costoletas de cordeiro** seencoo cooshtoolet-ash der coorday-roo

You may also want:

A chicken	**Um frango** oom frangoo
A rabbit	**Um coelho** oom co-ayl-yoo
A tongue	**Uma língua** ooma leengwa

Other essential expressions [*see also p. 56*]:

Please can you . . .	**Pode . . .** pod . . .
mince it?	**picá-lo?** peekah-loo
dice it?	**cortá-lo aos bocados?** coortah-loo ah-oosh boocah-doosh
trim the fat?	**tirar a gordura?** teerar ah goordoora

Fish

ESSENTIAL INFORMATION

- Fresh fish can be bought at the market (**mercado** or **praça**), or at the fish auctions (**lotas**) held on the fishing beaches.
- It can occasionally be found in the larger supermarkets too.
- Look for: **PEIXE** (fish) **PEIXARIA** (fishmonger's)
- Weight guide: 8 oz/ 250 g minimum per person, for one meal, of fish bought on the bone. i.e.

½ kilo/500 g	for 2 people
1 kilos	for 4 people
1½ kilos	for 6 people

WHAT TO SAY

Purchase large fish and small shellfish by the weight:

½ kilo of . . .	**Meio quilo de . . .**
	may-oo keeloo der . . .
1 kilo of . . .	**Um quilo de . . .**
	oom keeloo der . . .
1½ kilos of . . .	**Um quilo e meio de . . .**
	oom keeloo ee may-oo der . . .
cod	**bacalhau**
	bacal-yah-oo
whiting	**pescada**
	pshcah-da
dover sole	**linguado**
	leengwah-doo
sea-bream	**pargo**
	pargoo
shrimps	**camarões**
	camarownsh
prawns	**gambas**
	gambash
mussels	**mexilhões**
	mesheel-yownsh
sardines	**sardinhas**
	sardeen-yash
squid	**lulas**
	loolash
small saurel	**carapau**
	carapah-oo

Some large fish can be purchased by the slice:

One slice of . . .	**Um filete de . . .**
	oom feelet der . . .
Two slices of . . .	**Dois filetes de . . .**
	doysh feeletsh der . . .
Six slices of . . .	**Seis filetes de . . .**
	saysh feeletsh der . . .

salmon	**salmão**
	salmown
cod	**bacalhau**
	bacal-yah-oo
halibut	**alibute**
	aleeboot
fresh tuna	**atum**
	atoom

For some shellfish and 'frying pan' fish, specify the number:

A crab, please	**Um caranguejo, por favor**
	oom carangay-joo poor favor
A lobster	**Uma lagosta**
	ooma lagawshta
A female crab	**Uma santola**
	ooma santol-a
A big lobster	**Um lavagante**
	oom lavagant
A trout	**Uma truta**
	ooma troota
A sole	**Um linguado**
	oom leengwah-doo
A mackerel	**Uma cavala**
	ooma caval-a
A hake	**Uma garoupa**
	ooma garawpa

Other essential expressions [*see also p. 56*]:

Please can you . . .	**Pode . . . por favor?**
	pod . . . poor favor
take the heads off?	**tirar as cabeças**
	teerar ash cabessash
clean them?	**limpar**
	leempar
fillet them?	**cortar em filetes**
	coortar aim feeletsh

Eating and drinking out

Ordering a drink

ESSENTIAL INFORMATION

- The place to ask for: **UM CAFÉ** [*see p. 20*]
- By law, the price list of drinks (**TARIFAS DE CONSUMO**) must be displayed outside or in the window.
- There is waiter service in all cafés, but you can drink at the bar or counter if you wish – same price, but no service charge.
- Always leave a tip of 10% to 15% unless you see **SERVIÇO INCLUÍDO** (service included) printed on the bill or on a notice.
- Cafés serve non-alcoholic drinks and alcoholic drinks, and are normally open all day.
- Most cafés and 'beer houses' (**CERVEJARIAS**) also serve reasonably priced snacks and some also have a good à la carte service.
- A number of popular local 'nibbles' are often served free with beer/lager: **tremoços** (lupin seeds), **pevides** (salted and dried pumpkin seeds) and **favas ricas** (salted and fried broad beans).
- It is best to drink Portuguese tea on its own as milk impairs its flavour.

WHAT TO SAY

I'll have . . . please	**Queria . . . por favor** ker*ee*-a . . . poor fav*o*r
a small expresso black coffee	**uma bica** *oo*ma b*ee*ca
a small milky coffee	**um garoto** oom gar*a*wtoo
a diluted black coffee	**um carioca** oom caree-*o*ca
a large milky coffee	**um galão** oom gal*o*wn
a tea	**um chá** oom shah
with milk	**com leite** com late
with lemon	**com limão** com leem*o*wn

a glass of milk	**um copo de leite**
	oom k*o*poo der late
two glasses of milk	**dois copos de leite**
	doysh k*o*poosh der late
a hot chocolate	**um chocolate quente**
	oom shookool*a*t kent
a mineral water	**uma água mineral**
	*oo*ma *a*h-gwa meener*a*l
a lemonade (fizzy)	**uma limonada (com gás)**
	*oo*ma leemoon*a*da (com gash)
a Coca-Cola	**uma Coca Cola**
	*oo*ma coca-cola
an orangeade (fizzy)	**uma laranjada (com gás)**
	*oo*ma laranj*a*da (com gash)
an orange juice	**um sumo de laranja**
	oom s*oo*moo der lar*a*nja
a grape juice	**um sumo de uva**
	oom s*oo*moo der *oo*va
a pineapple juice	**um sumo de ananás**
	oom s*oo*moo der anan*a*sh
a fruit milkshake	**um batido de fruta**
	oom bat*ee*doo der fr*oo*ta
a lager	**uma cerveja**
	*oo*ma serv*ay*-ja
a glass of draught lager	**uma imperial**
	*oo*ma eemperee-*a*l
a pint of draught lager	**uma caneca**
	*oo*ma kan*e*ka
a brown ale	**uma cerveja preta**
	*oo*ma serv*ay*-ja pr*e*ta
A glass of . . .	**Um copo de . . .**
	oom c*o*poo der . . .
Two glasses of . . .	**Dois copos de . . .**
	doysh c*o*poosh der . . .
red wine	**vinho tinto**
	v*ee*n-yoo t*ee*ntoo
white wine	**vinho branco**
	v*ee*n-yoo br*a*ncoo
rosé wine	**vinho rosé**
	v*ee*n-yoo rozeh
dry/sweet	**seco/doce**
	seh-coo/daws

A bottle of . . .	**Uma garrafa de . . .**
	*oo*ma garr*a*fa der . . .
sparkling wine	**espumante**
	shpoom*a*nt
champagne	**champanhe**
	shamp*a*n-ye
A whisky	**Um whisky**
	oom oo-*ee*skee
with water	**com água**
	com *a*h-gwa
with ice	**com gêlo**
	com j*ai*loo
with soda	**com soda**
	com s*o*da
A gin	**Um gin**
	oom geem
and tonic	**com tónico**
	com t*o*neekoo
with lemon	**com limão**
	com leem*ow*n
A brandy/cognac	**Um brandy/cognac**
	oom brandy/cognac

These are local drinks you may like to try:

um capilé	cold, weak coffee with lemon
oom capeel*eh*	
um carioca de limão	lemon drink made by pouring
oom caree-*o*ca der leem*ow*n	boiling water on lemon peel
uma groselha	redcurrant drink
*oo*ma groz*ay*-la	
vinho verde	dry 'green' wine
v*ee*n-yoo v*a*ird	
ginginha	bitter-cherry liqueur
jeen-j*ee*n-ya	
licor Beirão	local-blend liqueur
leek*o*ar bayr*ow*n	
medronho de mel	blend of local firewater
medr*aw*n-yoo de mel	with honey
aguardente	aquavite
agwar-d*e*nt	
bagaço	firewater
bag*a*ssoo	

vinho do Porto   port
veen-yoo doo portoo
vinho da Madeira   Madeira
veen-yoo da maday-ra

Other essential expressions:

The bill, please   **A conta, por favor**
                            a conta poor favor

How much does that come to? **Quanto é tudo junto?**
                            kwantoo eh toodoo joontoo

Is service included?   **Tem serviço incluído?**
                            taim serveessoo eencloo-eedoo

Where is the toilet, please? **Onde é a casa de banho?**
                            awnd eh a cah-za der bain-yoo

Ordering a snack

ESSENTIAL INFORMATION

- Look for a café or bar with these signs:
  SNACK (snacks)
  COMIDAS (food)
  SANDES (sandwiches)
- In some regions mobile vans do hot snacks.
- For cakes, see p. 62
- For ice-cream, see p. 64
- For picnic-type snacks, see p. 69

WHAT TO SAY

I'll have . . . please	Queria . . . por favor
	ker*ee*-a . . . poor fav*o*r
a cheese sandwich	**uma sandes de queijo**
	*oo*ma sandsh der c*ay*-joo
a ham sandwich	**uma sandes de fiambre**
	*oo*ma sandsh der fee-*a*mbr
a cheese and ham sandwich	**uma sandes mista**
	*oo*ma sandsh m*ee*shta

These are some other snacks you may like to try:

uma sandes de paio	a garlic sausage sandwich
*oo*ma sandsh der pah-*ee*-oo	
um cachorro	a hot dog
oom cash*aw*-rroo	
um prego	a hot beefsteak roll
oom pr*e*g-oo	
uma bifana	a hot pork steak roll
*oo*ma beef*a*na	
uma sandes de presunto	a local parma-type ham sandwich
*oo*ma sandsh der prez*oo*ntoo	
um bitoque	a small steak with fried egg and
oom beet*o*c	chips
um pacote de batatas fritas	a packet of crisps
oom pac*o*t der bat*a*tash fr*ee*tash	

uma tosta	a toasted sandwhich
*oo*ma t*o*sh-ta	
uma tosta mista	cheese and ham toasted sandwich
*oo*ma t*o*sh-ta m*ee*shta	
um chouriço assado	a roasted garlic sausage
oom shawr*ee*ssoo ass*ah*-doo	
uma dose de mariscos	a portion of shellfish
*oo*ma d*o*z deh mar*ee*sh-coosh	

Some snacks, e.g. crisps and shellfish, may be sold at a variety of prices. You should add to the order:

20 escudos' worth of . . .	**Vinte escudos de . . .**
	veent shk*oo*doosh der . . .
100 escudos' worth of . . .	**Cem escudos de . . .**
	saym shk*oo*doosh der . . .

[*For other essential expressions, see 'Ordering a drink', p. 80*]

In a restaurant

ESSENTIAL INFORMATION

- The place to ask for: **UM RESTAURANTE** [see p. 20]
- You can eat at these places:
  RESTAURANTE
  CAFÉ
  CERVEJARIA (beer house)
  SNACK BAR
  SELF-SERVICE
  ESTALAGEM (quality inn)
  POUSADA (state owned inn)
- By law, the menus must be displayed outside or in the window – and that is the *only* way to judge if a place is right for your needs.
- Self-service exists, but most places have waiter service.
- Tip approximately 10% unless service is included.
- Half portions (**meia dose**) can be ordered for adults as well as children.
- Eating times are flexible – approximately 12.00 p.m. to 3.00 p.m. and 7.00 p.m. to 11.00 p.m.

WHAT TO SAY

May I book a table?	**Posso reservar uma mesa?**
	possoo rezairvar ooma mez-a
I've booked a table	**Tenho uma mesa reservada**
	tain-yoo ooma mez-a rezairvah-da
A table . . .	**Uma mesa . . .**
	ooma mez-a . . .
for one	**para uma pessoa**
	para ooma psaw-a
for three	**para três pessoas**
	para tresh psaw-ash
The à la carte menu, please	**O menu à la carte, por favor**
	oo mehnoo ah la cart poor favor
The fixed-price menu	**O menu de preço fixo**
	oo mehnoo der pressoo feecsoo
The tourist menu	**O menu turístico**
	oo mehnoo tooreeshticoo

Today's special menu	**Os pratos do dia** oosh prat-oosh doo dee-a
What's this, please? [*point to menu*]	**O que é isto, por favor?** oo ker eh eeshtoo poor favor
The wine list	**A lista dos vinhos** a leeshta doosh veen-yoosh
A carafe of wine, please	**Um jarro de vinho, por favor** oom jarroo der veen-yoo poor favor
A half (500 cc)	**Meio jarro** may-oo jarroo
A glass	**Um copo** oom cop-oo
A bottle	**Uma garrafa** ooma garrafa
A half-bottle	**Meia garrafa** may-a garrafa
A litre	**Um litro** oom leetroo
Red/white/rosé/house wine	**Vinho da casa tinto/branco/rosé** veen-yoo da cah-za teentoo/ brancoo/rozeh
Some more bread, please	**Mais pão, por favor** mah-eesh pown poor favor
Some more wine	**Mais vinho** mah-eesh veen-yoo
Some oil	**Óleo** ol-ee-oo
Some olive oil	**Azeite** azayt
Some vinegar	**Vinagre** veenagr
Some salt	**Sal** sahl
Some pepper	**Pimenta** peementa
Some water	**Água** ah-gwa
How much does that come to?	**Quanto é tudo?** kwantoo eh toodoo
Is service included?	**Tem serviço incluído?** taim serveessoo eencloo-eedoo
Where is the toilet, please?	**A casa de banho, por favor?** a cah-za der bain-yoo poor favor

The bill, please	**A conta, por favor**
	a conta poor favor
Can you give me a receipt?	**Pode-me dar um recibo?**
	pod-meh dar oom reseeboo

Key words for courses, as seen on some menus: [*Only ask this question if you want the waiter to remind you of the choice*]

What have you got in the way of . . .	**O que tem de . . .**
	oo ker taim der . . .
STARTERS?	**ENTRADAS?**
	entrah-dash
SOUP?	**SOPA?**
	sawpa
EGG DISHES?	**OVOS?**
	ovoosh
FISH?	**PEIXE?**
	paysh
MEAT?	**CARNE?**
	carn
GAME?	**CAÇA?**
	cassa
FOWL?	**AVES?**
	ahvsh
VEGETABLES?	**LEGUMES?**
	legoomsh
CHEESE?	**QUEIJO?**
	cay-joo
FRUIT?	**FRUTA?**
	froota
ICE-CREAM?	**GELADOS?**
	gelah-doosh
DESSERT?	**SOBREMESA?**
	sawbr-meza

UNDERSTANDING THE MENU

- You will find the names of the principal ingredients of most dishes on these pages:

Starters see p. 69   Fruit see p. 72
Meat see p. 75   Dessert see p. 62
Fish see p. 78   Cheese see p. 71
Vegetables see p. 73   Ice-cream see p. 64

- Used together with the following lists of cooking and menu terms, they should help you to decode the menu.
- The following cooking and menu terms are for understanding only – not for speaking aloud.

Cooking and menu terms

em açorda	in breadcrumbs (but not fried)
à alentejana	with garlic, clams and coriander
com alho	with garlic
assado	roasted
com azeite	with olive oil
bem passado	well done
na brasa	barbecued
à Bráz	with onions and potatoes in egg
à Bulhão-Pato	with garlic, olive oil and coriander
caldo	broth
na cataplana	cooked on a griddle
no churrasco	on the spit
com coentros	with fresh coriander
cozido	boiled
cozido a vapor	steamed
cru	raw
doce	sweet
de escabeche	marinated
escalfado	poached
à espanhola	with onions and tomato
no espeto	on the spit
estrelado	fried (egg)
estufado	cooked in its own juices
fervido	boiled
no forno	in the oven
frio	cold
frito	fried

fumado	smoked
em geleia	in aspic
à Gomes de Sá	with olives, potatoes and egg
gratinado	au gratin
guisado	stewed
com limão	with lemon
com Madeira	with Madeira
com manteiga	with butter
médio	medium done
meio cru	rare
mexido	scrambled
com molho	with sauce
com molho da casa	with the house sauce
com molho de vinagrete	with vinaigrette sauce
com molho picante	with spicy sauce
ao natural	plain
com ovo a cavalo	with fried egg on top
panado	fried in breadcrumbs
passado por água	blanched
à portuguesa	with tomatoes, onions, olive oil
recheado	stuffed
com salsa	with parsley
salteado	sautéed
com tinta	in its own ink (squid)
com tomate	with tomato
à transmontana	with cabbage

Further words to help you understand the menu

açorda à alentejana	very rich coriander soup with egg and bread
almôndegas	meatballs
ameijoas à Bulhão-Pato	clams in garlic sauce
arroz à portuguesa	vegetable rice
bacalhau	salted dried cod served in numerous ways
bife	steak
borrego	lamb
cabrito	kid
caranguejo	crab
carne de porco à alentejana	pork with clams
carnes frias	cold meats

chispalhada	pigs' trotters stew
chocos com tinta	squid in their own ink
codornizes	quail
coelho guisado	stewed rabbit
dobrada	tripe stew
empadas de galinha	chicken pies
enchidos	garlic sausages
ervilhas guisadas	stewed peas
favas	broad beans
feijoada	bean and sausage stew
fígado	liver
gambas al ajilho	king prawns fried in olive oil with garlic
gaspacho	cold vegetable soup (usually tomato)
linguado	dover sole
lulas	squid
mexilhão	mussels
miolos	brains
pastéis de massa folhada	vol-au-vents
peixe espada	swordfish
peixinhos da horta	runner beans in batter
perdizes	partridges
perna de porco	leg of pork
pombo	pigeon
rins	kidneys
salada de atum	tuna salad
salsichas	sausages
sopa de marisco	shellfish soup
torta	type of Swiss roll sponge with filling
tripas	tripe

Health

ESSENTIAL INFORMATION

- For details of reciprocal health agreements between your country and the country you are visiting, visit your local Department of Health office at least one month before leaving, or ask your travel agent.
- Take your own 'first line' first aid kit with you.
- For minor disorders and treatment at a chemist's, see p. 42.
- For finding your way to a doctor, dentist or chemist's, see p. 20.
- Once in the country, decide on a definite plan of action in case of serious illness: communicate your problem to a near neighbour, the receptionist or someone you see regularly. You are then dependent on that person helping you obtain treatment.
- In an emergency, dial 115 for the ambulance service.

What's the matter?

I have a pain . . .	**Tenho uma dor . . .**
	tain-yoo *oo*ma d*o*r
in my abdomen	**de barriga**
	der bahrr*ee*ga
in my ankle	**no tornozelo**
	noo toornooz*e*loo
in my arm	**no braço**
	noo br*a*ssoo
in my back	**nas costas**
	nash c*o*shtash
in my bladder	**na bexiga**
	na besh*ee*ga
in my bowels	**nos intestinos**
	noosh eentesh-t*ee*noosh
in my breast	**no peito**
	noo p*a*ytoo
in my chest	**no peito**
	noo p*a*ytoo
in my ear	**no ouvido**
	noo awv*ee*doo
in my eye	**no olho**
	noo *o*l-yoo

in my foot	**no pé**
	noo p*e*h
in my head	**na cabeça**
	na cab*e*ssa
in my heel	**no calcanhar**
	noo calcan-y*a*r
in my kidney	**no rim**
	noo r*ee*m
in my leg	**na perna**
	na p*air*na
in my lung	**no pulmão**
	noo poolm*ow*n
in my neck	**no pescoço**
	noo pesh-k*a*wsoo
in my penis	**no pénis**
	noo p*e*n-eesh
in my shoulder	**no ombro**
	noo *a*wmbroo
in my stomach	**no estômago**
	noo sht*a*wmagoo
in my testicle	**no testículo**
	noo tesht*ee*cooloo
in my throat	**na garganta**
	na g*a*rganta
in my vagina	**na vagina**
	na vaj*ee*na
in my wrist	**no pulso**
	noo p*oo*lsoo
I have a pain here [*point*]	**Tenho uma dor aqui**
	t*ai*n-yoo *oo*ma dor ak*ee*
I have a toothache	**Tenho uma dor de dentes**
	t*ai*n-yoo *oo*ma dor der d*e*ntsh
I have broken . . .	**Parti . . .**
	part*ee* . . .
my dentures	**a minha dentadura**
	ah m*ee*n-ya dentad*oo*ra
my glasses	**os meus óculos**
	oosh m*e*h-oosh *o*cooloosh
I have lost . . .	**Perdi . . .**
	perd*ee* . . .
my contact lenses	**as minhas lentes de contacto**
	ash m*ee*n-yash l*e*ntsh der cont*a*ctoo
a filling	**um chumbo**
	oom sh*oo*mboo

My child is ill	**O meu filho/a minha filha está doente** oo meh-oo feel-yoo/a meen-ya feel-ya shtah doo-ent
He/she has a pain in	**Ele/ela tem uma dor** el/el-a taim ooma dor
his/her . . .	**no seu/na sua . . .** noo seh-oo/na soo-a . . .
ankle [see list above]	**tornozelo** toornoozelloo

How bad is it?

I'm ill	**Estou doente** shtaw doo-ent
It's urgent	**É urgente** eh oorgent
It's serious	**É sério** eh sairee-oo
It's not serious	**Não é sério** nown eh sairee-oo
It hurts (a lot)	**Dói (muito)** doy (moo-eetoo)
It doesn't hurt much	**Não dói muito** nown doy moo-eetoo
The pain occurs . . .	**A dor acontece . . .** a dor acontess . . .
every quarter of an hour	**de quarto em quarto de hora** der kwartoo aim kwartoo der ora
every half-hour	**de meia em meia hora** der may-a aim may-a ora
every hour	**de hora em hora** der ora aim ora
every day	**todos os dias** tawdoosh oosh dee-ash
most of the time	**a maior parte do tempo** ah may-or part doo tempoo
I've had it for . . .	**Já a tenho há . . .** jah ah tain-yoo ah . . .
one hour/one day	**uma hora/um dia** ooma ora/oom dee-a
two hours/two days	**duas horas/dois dias** doo-ash orash/doysh dee-ash

It's a . . .	É uma . . .
	eh *oo*ma . . .
sharp pain	**dor aguda**
	dor ag*oo*da
dull ache	**dor contínua**
	dor cont*ee*noo-a
nagging pain	**dor constante**
	dor consh-t*ant*
I feel . . .	Sinto-me . . .
	s*ee*ntoo-meh . . .
dizzy	**tonto/a***
	t*aw*ntoo/a
sick	**enjoado/a***
	enjoo-*ah*-doo/a
weak	**sem forças**
	saym f*aw*rsash
feverish	**com febre**
	com febr

Already under treatment for something else?

I take . . . regularly [*show*]	**Tomo . . . regularmente**
,	t*o*moo . . . regoolarm*ent*
this medicine	**este medicamento**
	*e*sht medeecam*e*ntoo
these pills	**estes comprimidos**
	eshtsh compreem*ee*doosh
I have . . .	Sofro . . .
	s*a*wfroo . . .
a heart condition	**do coração**
	doo coorass*ow*n
haemorrhoids	**das hemorroidas**
	dash *e*m-oorroydash
rheumatism	**de reumático**
	der r*e*h-oom*a*ticoo
I am . . .	Sou . . .
	saw . . .
diabetic	**diabético/a***
	dee-ab*e*tico/a
asthmatic	**asmático/a***
	ash-m*a*ticoo/a

*First alternative for men, second for women.

I am . . .
Sou . . .
saw . . .

allergic to penicillin
alérgico/a à penicilina*
al*ai*rjicoo/a ah penee-seel*ee*na

I am pregnant
Estou grávida
shtaw gr*av-ee*da

Other essential expressions

Please can you help?
Pode ajudar-me por favor?
pod aj*oo*d*a*r-meh poor fav*o*r

A doctor please
Um médico por favor
oom m*e*dicoo poor fav*o*r

A dentist
Um dentista
oom dent*ee*shta

I don't speak Portuguese
Não falo português
nown f*a*h-loo poortoog*e*sh

What time does . . . arrive?
A que horas chega . . .
ah ker *o*rash sh*e*g-a . . .

the doctor
o médico?
oo m*e*dicoo

the dentist
o dentista?
oo dent*ee*shta

From the doctor: key sentences to understand

Take this . . .
Tome isto . . .
tom *ee*shtoo . . .

every day/hour
todos os dias/de hora em hora
t*a*wdoosh oosh d*ee*-ash/der *o*ra aim *o*ra

twice/three times a day
duas/três vezes ao dia
d*oo*ash/tresh v*e*hzsh ao d*ee*a

Stay in bed
Fique na cama
feek na c*a*h-ma

Don't travel . . .
Não viaje . . .
nown vee-*a*j . . .

for . . . days/weeks
por . . . dias/semanas
poor . . . d*ee*-ash/sem*a*h-nash

You must go to hospital
Tem que dar entrada no hospital
taim ker dar entr*a*h-da noo ohsh-peet*a*l

---

*First alternative for men, second for women.

Problems: complaints, loss, theft

ESSENTIAL INFORMATION

● Problems with:
camping facilities, see p. 36
household appliances, see p. 54
health, see p. 92
the car, see p. 106
● If the worst comes to the worst, find the police station.
To ask the way, see p. 20.
Look for:
POLÍCIA
GNR (Guarda Nacional Republicana – National Guard)
● If you lose your passport go to your nearest Consulate
● In an emergency, dial 322222 (Fire) or 364141/372131 (Police)

COMPLAINTS

I bought this . . .	**Comprei isto . . .** cawnpr*ay ee*shtoo . . .
today	**hoje** awj
yesterday	**ontem** *a*wntaim
on Monday [*see p. 130*]	**na segunda-feira** na seg*oo*nda f*a*yra
It's no good	**Não serve** nown sairv
Look	**Olhe** *o*l-yer
Here [*point*]	**Aqui** ak*ee*
Can you . . .	**Pode . . .** pod . . .
change it?	**trocá-lo?** troo*cah*-loo
mend it?	**repará-lo?** repar*ah*-loo
give me a refund	**me reembolsar?** meh ree-embawls*a*r

Here's the receipt	**Tem aqui o recibo**
	taim ak*ee* oo ress*ee*boo
Can I see the manager?	**Posso ver o gerente?**
	p*o*ssoo vair oo jer*e*nt

LOSS
[*See also 'Theft' below: the lists are interchangeable*]

I have lost . . .	**Perdi . . .**
	perd*ee*
my bag	**a minha mala**
	ah m*ee*n-ya m*a*h-la
my bracelet	**a minha pulseira**
	ah m*ee*n-ya pools*ay*-ra
my camera	**a minha máquina fotográfica**
	ah m*ee*nya m*a*c-eena footoografeeca
my car keys	**as chaves do meu carro**
	ash sh*a*vsh doo m*e*h-oo c*a*rroo
my car logbook	**o livrete do meu carro**
	oo l*ee*vret doo m*e*h-oo c*a*rroo
my driving licence	**a minha carta de condução**
	ah m*ee*n-ya c*a*rta der cawndoos*o*wn
my insurance certificate	**o meu certificado de seguro**
	oo m*e*h-oo serteefee-c*a*h-do der seg*oo*roo
my jewellery	**as minhas jóias**
	ash m*ee*n-yash j*o*y-ash
everything!	**tudo!**
	t*oo*doo

THEFT
[*See also 'Loss' above: the lists are interchangeable*]

Someone has stolen . . .	**Roubaram-me . . .**
	rawbar*o*wn meh . . .
my car	**o meu carro**
	oo m*e*h-oo c*a*rroo
my car radio	**o rádio do meu carro**
	oo r*a*dee-oo doo m*e*h-oo c*a*rroo
my keys	**as minhas chaves**
	ash m*ee*n-yash sh*a*vsh

my luggage	**a minha bagagem**
	ah meen-ya bagajaim
my money	**o meu dinheiro**
	oo meh-oo deen-yay-roo
my necklace	**o meu colar**
	oo meh-oo coolar
my passport	**o meu passaporte**
	oo meh-oo passaport
my purse	**o meu porta-moedas**
	oo meh-oo porta-mooedash
my radio	**o meu rádio**
	oo meh-oo radee-oo
my tickets	**os meus bilhetes**
	oosh meh-oosh beel-yetsh
my travellers' cheques	**os meus travellers' cheques**
	oosh meh-oosh travellers sheh-ksh
my wallet	**a minha carteira**
	ah meen-ya cartay-ra
my watch	**o meu relógio**
	oo meh-oo relojee-oo

LIKELY REACTIONS: key words to understand

Wait	**Espere**
	shpair
When?	**Quando?**
	kwandoo
Where?	**Onde?**
	awnd
Name?	**Nome?**
	nawm
Address?	**Morada?**
	moorah-da
I can't help you	**Não o posso ajudar**
	nown oo possoo ajoodar
Nothing to do with me	**Não é nada comigo**
	nown eh nah-da coomeegoo

The post office

ESSENTIAL INFORMATION

- To find a post office, see p. 20
- Key words to look for:
  CORREIOS
  CTT – CORREIOS, TELEGRAFOS E TELEFONES
- Look for the letters **CTT** on a blue sign
- For stamps look for the word: **SELOS**
- Mailboxes are red.
- For poste-restante, you should show your passport at the counter marked **POSTE RESTANTE**: a small fee is usually payable.

WHAT TO SAY

To England, please	**Para Inglaterra, por favor**
	para eenglatairra poor favor

[*Hand letters, cards or parcels over the counter*]

To Australia	**Para a Austrália**
	para a ah-oosh-trahlia
To the United States	**Para os Estados Unidos**
	para oosh shtah-doosh ooneedoosh

[*For other countries, see p. 134*]

How much is . . .	**Quanto é . . .**
	kwantoo eh
this parcel (to Canada)?	**esta encomenda (para o Canadá)?**
	eshta aincoo-menda (para oo canadah)
a letter (to Australia)?	**uma carta (para a Austrália)?**
	ooma carta (para aah-oosh-trahlia)
a postcard (to England)?	**um postal (para Inglaterra)?**
	oom pooshtal (para eenglatairra)

Airmail	**Por avião**
	poor avee-*o*wn
Surface mail	**Por terra**
	poor t*ai*rra
One stamp, please	**Um selo, por favor**
	oom s*e*l-oo poor fav*o*r
Two stamps	**Dois selos**
	doysh s*e*l-oosh
One 10$00 stamp	**Um selo de dez escudos**
	oom s*e*l-oo der dej shk*oo*doosh
I'd like to send a telegram	**Queria enviar um telegrama**
	ker*ee*-a envee-*a*r oom telegr*a*ma

Telephoning

ESSENTIAL INFORMATION

- Unless you read and speak Portuguese well, it's best not to make phone calls by yourself. Go to a post office (or bar) and write the town and number you want on a piece of paper. Add **COM PRÉ-AVISO** if you want a person-to-person call or **PARA SER PAGA PELO DESTINATARIO** if you want to reverse the charges.
- There are two types of public phones in Portugal — the first, and most common, are in booths and take $50 and 1$00 coins which you feed into the machine once the number you have dialled has answered. The second type is a red phone, commonly found in cafés. Here you have to feed your coins in first before you can get a dial tone — any coins left after speaking that have not been used up and returned to you.
- For the UK dial 0744 and the number you require.
- For the USA dial 17 and ask the operator for the number you require.
- Tourist Information (in English) is available on this number in Lisbon: 706341.

WHAT TO SAY

Where can I make a telephone call? **Onde posso fazer uma chamada?**
awnd *p*osso faz*air* *oo*ma sham*ah*-da
Local/abroad **Local/para fora**
loo*cal*/*p*ara *f*ora

I'd like this number . . . **Queria este número . . .**
ker*ee*-a esht n*oo*meroo . . .
[*show number*]
in England **na Inglaterra**
na eenglat*air*ra

in Canada **no Canadá**
noo canad*ah*

in the USA **nos Estados Unidos**
noosh sht*ah*-doosh oon*ee*doosh
[*For other countries, see p. 134*]

Can you dial it for me, please? **Podia-me marcar por favor?**
poodee-a-meh marcar poor favor

How much is it? **Quanto custa?**
kwantoo cooshta

Hello? **Está?**
shtah

May I speak to . . .? **Posso falar com . . . ?**
possoo falar com . . .

Extension . . . **A extensão . . .**
a shtensown . . .

I'm sorry, I don't speak Portuguese **Desculpe, não falo português**
deshcoolp nown fah-lo poortoogesh

Do you speak English? **Fala inglês?**
fah-la eenglesh

Thank you, I'll phone back **Muito obrigado/a, eu volto a telefonar***
moo-eetoo obreegah-doo/a eh-oo voltoo a telefoonar

Goodbye **Adeus**
adeh-oosh

LIKELY REACTIONS

That's . . . **São . . .**
sown . . .

Cabin number (3) *[For numbers, see p. 126]* **Na cabine número (três)**
na cabeen noomeroo (tresh)

Don't hang up **Não desligue**
nown deshleeg

I'm trying to connect you **Estou a tentar fazer a ligação**
shtaw ah tentar fazair a leegassown

You're through **Pode falar**
pod falar

There's a delay **Está atrasado**
shtah atrazah-doo

I'll try again **Volto a tentar**
voltoo a taintar

*First alternative for men, second for women.

Changing checks and money

ESSENTIAL INFORMATION

- Finding your way to a bank or change bureau, see p. 20.
- Look for these words on buildings:
  BANCO (bank)
  CRÉDITO
  CÂMBIO-EXCHANGE (change bureau)
- To cash your own normal checks, exactly as at home, use your credit card where you see the Eurocheque sign.
- Banks are open between 8.30 a.m. and 12.00 p.m. and 1.00 p.m. and 2.30 p.m. except on Saturdays and Sundays. A currency exchange service is usually available all day during the high season.
- Have your passport handy.

WHAT TO SAY

I'd like to cash . . .

Queria trocar . . .
ker*ee*-a troo*car* . . .

this travellers' cheque

este cheque de viagem
esht shek de vee-*a*jaim

this cheque

este cheque
esht shek

I'd like to change this into Portuguese escudos

Queria trocar isto por escudos portugueses
ker*ee*-a troo*car eesh*too poor sh*koo*doosh poortoogezesh

Here's . . .

Aqui tem . . .
ak*ee* taim . . .

my banker's card

o meu cartão bancário
oo m*eh*-oo cart*own* banc*aree*-oo

my passport

o meu passaporte
oo m*eh*-oo passa*port*

For excursions into neighbouring countries

I'd like to change this . . .　　**Queria trocar isto . . .**
　[*show bank notes*]　　ker*ee*-a tro*ocar* *ee*shtoo . . .
　into French francs　　**por francos franceses**
　　　　poor fr*a*ncoosh frans*ez*-esh

　into Spanish pesetas　　**por pesetas espanholas**
　　　　poor pez*et*-ash shpan-y*o*l-ash

What's the rate of exchange?　　**Qual é o câmbio corrente?**
　　　　kwal eh o c*a*mbee-oo coorrent

LIKELY REACTIONS

Your passport, please　　**O seu passaporte, por favor**
　　　　oo s*e*h-oo passap*o*rt poor fav*o*r

Sign here　　**Assine aqui**
　　　　ass*ee*n ak*ee*

Your banker's card, please　　**O seu cartão bancário, por favor**
　　　　oo s*e*h-oo cart*ow*n banc*a*ree-oo
　　　　poor fav*o*r

Go to the cash desk　　**Vá à caixa**
　　　　vah ah cah-*ee*sha

Car travel

ESSENTIAL INFORMATION

- Finding a filling station or garage, see p. 20.
- Grades of gasoline:
  SUPER
  NORMAL (2 star standard)
  DOIS TEMPOS (two stroke)
  GASÓLEO (diesel)
- 1 gallon is about 4½ litres (accurate enough up to 6 gallons).
- Types of garages: Often 'all in one' called **GARAGEM,** but sometimes separate under **BATE CHAPAS** (body repairs); **GARAGEM DE SERVIÇO** (mechanical repairs and service); **REPARAÇÕES ELÉCTRICAS** (for electrical faults); and **PNEUS** (tyres).
- Most garages are open 8.00 a.m. to 12.00 p.m. and 2.00 p.m. to 7.00 p.m. but not Saturdays. If driving inland, remember to fill up as gas stations may be closed or hard to find.
- Unfamiliar road signs and warnings, see p. 121.

WHAT TO SAY

[*For numbers, see p. 126*]

(9) litres of . . .	**(Nove) litros de . . .**
	(nov) le*e*troosh der . . .
(200) escudos of . . .	**(Duzentos) escudos de . . .**
	(doozentoosh) shk*oo*doosh der . . .
standard	**normal**
	norm*a*l
premium	**super**
	s*oo*per
diesel	**gasóleo**
	gaz*o*l-ee-oo
Fill it up, please	**Pode encher, por favor**
	pod *a*inchair poor fav*o*r

Will you check . . .	**Pode verificar . . .** pod vereefee*car* . . .
the oil?	**o nível do óleo?** oo *nee*vel doo *o*l-ee-oo
the battery?	**a água da bateria?** a *ah*-gwa da bater*ee*-a
the radiator?	**a água do radiador?** a *ah*-gwa doo radee-a*dor*
the tyres?	**a pressão dos pneus?** a press*own* doosh pneh-oosh
I've run out of petrol	**Acabou-se a gasolina** acab*aw*-seh a gazool*ee*na
Can I borrow a can, please?	**Pode emprestar-me uma lata, por favor** pod aimpresht*ar*-meh *oo*ma *lah*-ta poor fav*or*
My car has broken down	**O meu carro avariou-se** oo m*eh*-oo *carr*oo avar*ee*-*aw*s
My car won't start	**O meu carro não pega** oo m*eh*-oo *carr*oo n*own* p*eg*-a
I've had an accident	**Tive um acidente** t*ee*v oom asse*ed*ent
I've lost my car keys	**Perdi as chaves do meu carro** perd*ee* ash sh*a*vsh doo m*eh*-oo *carr*oo
My car is . . .	**O meu carro está . . .** oo m*eh*-oo *carr*oo sht*ah* . . .
two kilometres away	**a dois quilómetros daqui** ah d*oy*sh keelomtroosh dak*ee*
three kilometres away	**a três quilómetros daqui** ah tresh keelomtroosh dak*ee*
Can you help me, please?	**Pode ajudar-me, por favor?** pod aj*oo*dar-meh poor fav*or*
Do you do repairs?	**Faz reparações?** fash reparas*oy*nsh
I have a puncture?	**Tenho um pneu furado** t*ai*n-yoo oom pneh-oo foor*ah*-doo
I have a broken windscreen	**Tenho o pára-brisas partido** t*ai*n-yoo oo *para*-br*ee*zash part*ee*doo
I think the problem is here . . . [*point*]	**Penso que o problema está aqui . . .** p*en*soo ker oo prob*le*ma sht*ah* ak*ee* . . .

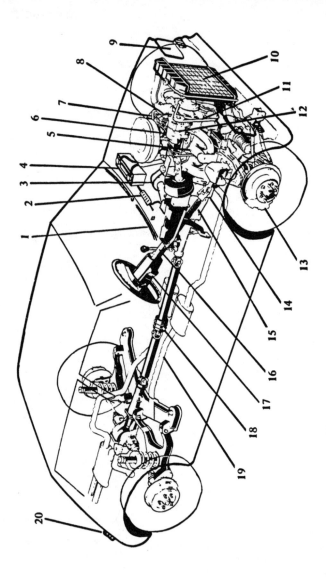

1	windscreen wipers	**os limpa pára-brisas**	oosh *leempa para-breezash*
2	fuses	**os fusíveis**	oosh *foosee-veish*
3	heater	**o aquecimento**	oo *akesseementoo*
4	battery	**a bateria**	a *bateree-a*
5	engine	**o motor**	oo *mootor*
6	fuel pump	**a bomba da gasolina**	a *bomba da gazooleena*
7	starter motor	**o motor de arranque**	oo *mootor der arrank*
8	carburettor	**o carburador**	oo *carboo-rador*
9	lights	**as luzes**	ash *loozsh*
10	radiator	**o radiador**	oo *radee-ador*
11	fan belt	**a correia da ventoinha**	a *coorray-a da ventoo-een-ya*
12	generator	**o dínamo**	oo *deenamoo*
13	brakes	**os travões**	oosh *travoynsh*
14	clutch	**a embraiagem**	a *aimbray-ajaim*
15	gear box	**a caixa de velocidades**	a *cah-eesha deh veloosseedadsh*
16	steering	**a direcção**	a *deeressown*
17	ignition	**a ignição**	a *eegneessown*
18	transmission	**a transmissão**	a *transh-meessown*
19	exhaust	**o tubo de escape**	oo *tooboo der shkap*
20	indicators	**os pisca-piscas**	oosh *peeshka-peeshkash*

I don't know what's wrong	**Não sei onde é a avaria** nown say awnd eh a avar*ee*-a
Can you . . .	**Pode . . .** pod . . .
repair the fault?	**reparar a avaria?** repar*ar* a avar*ee*-a
come and look?	**vir ver?** veer v*air*
estimate the cost?	**dar-me o orçamento?** d*ar*-meh oo orssam*en*too
write it down?	**escrevê-lo?** shkrev*eh*-loo
Do you accept these coupons?	**Aceita estes vales?** ass*ay*ta *e*shtesh valsh
How long will the repair take?	**Quanto tempo demora a reparar?** kw*an*too t*em*poo dem*o*ra a repar*ar*
When will the car be ready?	**Quando está pronto o carro?** kw*an*doo shtah pr*aw*ntoo oo c*ar*roo
This is my insurance document	**Isto é o documento do meu seguro** *ee*shtoo eh oo dooco*o*mentoo doo meh-oo seg*oo*roo

HIRING A CAR

Can I hire a car?	**Posso alugar um carro?** p*o*ssoo aloog*ar* oom c*ar*roo
I need a car . . .	**Preciso de um carro . . .** press*ee*zoo de oom c*ar*roo . . .
for two people	**para duas pessoas** p*ara* d*oo*-ash ps*aw*-ash
for five people	**para cinco pessoas** p*ara* s*een*coo ps*aw*-ash
for one day	**para um dia** p*ara* oom d*ee*-a
for five days	**para cinco dias** p*ara* s*een*coo d*ee*-ash
for a week	**para uma semana** p*ara* *oo*ma sem*ah*-na

Can you write down . . .   **Pode escrever . . .**
pod shkrev*air* . . .

the deposit to pay?   **o depósito a pagar?**
oo de*po*zeetoo a pag*a*r

the charge per kilometre?   **o preço por quilómetro?**
oo pr*e*ssoo poor keel*o*mtroo

the daily charge?   **o preço diário?**
oo pr*e*ssoo dee-*a*r-ee-oo

the cost of insurance?   **o preço do seguro?**
oo pr*e*ssoo doo seg*oo*roo

Can I leave it in (Lisbon)?   **Posso deixá-lo em (Lisboa)?**
*po*ssoo daysh*a*h-loo aim
(leeshb*oo*-a)

What documents do I need?   **Que documentos preciso?**
ker doocooment*oo*sh press*ee*zoo

LIKELY REACTIONS

I don't do repairs   **Não faço reparações**
nown f*a*ssoo reparas*oy*nsh

Where is your car?   **Onde está o seu carro?**
awnd shtah oo s*e*h-oo c*a*rroo

What make is it?   **De que marca é?**
der ker m*a*rca eh

Come back tomorrow/on   **Volte amanhã/na segunda-feira**
Monday   volt aman-y*a*n/na seg*oo*nda f*a*yra
[*For days of the week, see p. 130*]
We don't hire cars   **Não alugo carros**
nown al*oo*goo c*a*rroosh

Your driving licence, please   **A sua carta de condução, por favor**
a soo-a c*a*rta der cawndooss*ow*n
poor favor

The mileage is unlimited   **A quilometragem é ilimitada**
a keelom-traj*a*im eh eeleemeet*a*h-
da

Public transport

ESSENTIAL INFORMATION

- Finding the way to the bus station, a bus stop, a trolley stop, the railway station and a taxi stand, see p. 20.
- Lining up in Portugal can be haphazard.
- Taxi services operate as here in most main towns; in smaller towns, however, cars for hire which operate as taxis charge per kilometre. Hail a taxi as you would at home.
- There is a national train network. Frequent fast electric trains connect Lisbon with the tourist zones of Sintra and Cascais. The **CP** (Portuguese Railways) keep two steam trains in circulation during the high season for tourists.
- Long distance buses and coach services are reasonably frequent and cover most of the Portuguese provinces. In remote districts, however, buses may run irregularly.
- Lisbon is serviced by trams, buses and a small underground network. If you are spending a couple of days in the capital, buy a *tourist ticket* at any of the City Transport Company's information kiosks (they can only be used for surface public transport).
- Booklets of tickets are also available for subway travel — you will have to pay more if you buy each ticket separately.
- Key words on signs [*see also p. 121*]
  BILHETES (tickets)
  ENTRADA (entrance)
  PROIBIDO (forbidden)
  CAIS (platform)
  INFORMAÇÕES (information)
  SAÍDA (exit)
  DEPÓSITO DE BAGAGEM (left-luggage)
  PARAGEM DE AUTOCARRO (bus stop)
  HORÁRIO (timetable)

WHAT TO SAY

Where does the train for (Lisbon) leave from?	**De onde parte o comboio para (Lisboa)?** der awnd part oo comboy-oo para (leeshboo-a)
At what time does the train leave for (Lisbon)?	**A que horas parte o comboio para (Lisboa)?** a ker orash part oo comboy-oo para (leeshboo-a)
At what time does the train arrive in (Lisbon)?	**A que horas chega o comboio a (Lisboa)?** a ker orash sheg-a oo comboy-oo a (leeshboo-a)
Is this the train for (Lisbon)?	**É este o comboio para (Lisboa)?** eh esht oo comboy-oo para (leeshboo-a)
Where does the bus for (Coimbra) leave from?	**De onde parte a camioneta para (Coimbra)?** der awnd part a kam-yoonet-a para (coo-eembra)
At what time does the bus leave for (Coimbra)?	**A que horas parte a comioneta para (Coimbra)?** a ker orash part a kam-yoonet-a para (coo-eembra)
At what time does the bus arrive at (Coimbra)?	**A que horas chega a camioneta a (Coimbra)?** a ker orash sheg-a a kam-yoonet-a a (coo-eembra)
Is this the bus for (Coimbra)?	**É esta a camioneta para (Coimbra)?** eh eshta a kam-yoonet-a para (coo-eembra)
Do I have to change?	**Tenho que fazer mudança?** tain-yoo ker fazair moodansa
Where does . . . leave from?	**De onde parte . . .** der awnd part . . .
the bus	**o autocarro?** oo ah-ootoh-carroo
the train	**o comboio?** oo comboy-oo
the tram	**o eléctrico?** oo eeletreecoo

Where does . . . leave from? **De onde parte . . . ?**
der awnd part . . .

the underground **o metropolitano (metro)**
oo metro-pooleet*a*noo/*metroo*

for the airport **para o aeroporto**
p*a*ra oo airohp*o*rtoo

for the cathedral **para a catedral**
p*a*ra a catedr*a*l

for the beach **para a praia**
p*a*ra a pr*a*h-ya

for the market place **para a praça**
p*a*ra a pr*a*ssa

for the railway station **para a estação de comboios**
p*a*ra a shtass*o*wn der comb*o*y-oosh

for the town centre **para o centro da cidade**
p*a*ra oo s*e*ntroo da seed*a*d

for the town hall **para a câmara municipal**
p*a*ra a c*a*mara mooneeseep*a*l

for the São Roque church **para a igreja de São Roque**
p*a*ra a eegr*a*y-ja der sown rock

for the swimming pool **para a piscina**
p*a*ra a peesh-s*ee*na

Is this . . . **É este . . .**
eh esht . . .

the bus for the market place? **o autocarro para a praça?**
oo ah-ootoh-c*a*rroo p*a*ra a pr*a*ssa

the tram for the railway station? **o eléctrico para a estação?**
oo eel*e*tricoo p*a*ra a shtass*o*wn

Where can I get a taxi? **Onde posso arranjar um taxi?**
*a*wnd p*o*ssoo arranj*a*r oom t*a*xi

Can you put me off at the right stop, please? **Pode dizer-me onde devo descer, por favor?**
pod deez*ai*r-meh *a*wnd devoo desh-s*e*hr poor fav*o*r

Can I book a seat? **Posso reservar um lugar?**
p*o*ssoo rezerv*a*r oom loog*a*r

A single **Uma ida**
*oo*ma *ee*da

A return **Uma ida e volta**
*oo*ma *ee*da ee v*o*lta

First class **Em primeira classe**
aim preem*a*y-ra klas

Second class	**Em segunda classe** aim seg*oo*nda klas
One adult	**Para um adulto** p*a*ra oom ad*oo*ltoo
Two adults	**Para dois adultos** p*a*ra doysh ad*oo*ltoosh
and one child	**e uma criança** ee *oo*ma cree-*a*nsa
and two children	**e duas crianças** ee d*oo*-ash cree-*a*nsash
How much is it?	**Quanto custa?** kw*a*ntoo coosht*a*

LIKELY REACTIONS

Over there	**Ali** al*ee*
Here	**Aqui** ak*ee*
Platform (1)	**No cais número (um)** no c*a*h-eesh n*oo*meroo (oom)
At 16.00 [*For times, see p. 128*] Change at (Oeiras)	**Às dezasseis horas** ash dez-as*a*ysh *o*rash **Mude em (Oeiras)** mood aim (oo-*a*yrash)
Change at (the town hall)	**Mude no (largo da câmara)** mood noo (l*a*rgoo da c*a*mara)
This is your stop	**A sua paragem é esta** a s*oo*-a par*a*jaim eh *e*shta
There's only first class	**Só tem primeira classe** s*o* taim preem*ay*-ra klas
There's a supplement	**Tem sobretaxa** taim sawbr-t*a*sha

Leisure

ESSENTIAL INFORMATION

- Finding the way to a place of entertainment, see p. 20.
- For times of day, see p. 128.
- Important signs, see p. 121.
- Smoking is not permitted in movies, theatres, etc. during performances. You may, however, smoke during intervals, away from the seating area.
- Foreign films have subtitles and are not dubbed.
- Tip the usherettes approximately 5$00.
- The bullfight — be careful of black market ticket sellers as you may find that particular day is not the sell-out that they claim!

WHAT TO SAY

At what time does . . . open?	A que horas abre . . . ?
	a ker orash abr . . .
the art gallery	a galeria de arte
	a galeree-a der art
the botanical garden	o jardim botânico
	oo jardeem bootan-icoo
the cinema	o cinema
	oo seenem-a
the concert hall	a sala de concertos
	a sal-a der cawn-sairtoosh
the disco	a discoteca
	a deesh-cootec-a
the museum	o museu
	oo moozeh-oo
the night club	a 'boîte'
	a boo-at
the sports stadium	o estádio desportivo
	oo shtah-dee-oo deshpoorteevoo
the swimming pool	a piscina
	a peesh-seena
the theatre	o teatro
	oo tee-atroo
the zoo	o jardim zoológico
	oo jardeem zoolojicoo

At what time does . . . close?	**A que horas fecha . . .?**
	a ker *o*rash f*a*y-sha . . .
the art gallery	**a galeria de arte**
[*See above list*]	a galer*ee*-a der art
At what time does . . . start?	**A que horas começa . . .?**
	a ker *o*rash coom*e*ssa . . .
the cabaret	**o espectáculo**
	oo shpet*a*kooloo
the concert	**o concerto**
	oo cawn-s*ai*rtoo
the film	**o filme**
	oo feelm
the match	**o desafio/jogo**
	oo dezaf*ee*-oo/j*a*wgoo
the play	**a peça**
	a p*e*ssa
the race	**a corrida**
	a coorr*ee*da
How much is it . . .	**Quanto é . . .**
	kw*a*ntoo eh . . .
for an adult?	**para um adulto?**
	p*a*ra oom ad*oo*ltoo
for a child?	**para uma criança?**
	p*a*ra *oo*ma cree-*a*nsa
Two adults, please	**Dois adultos, por favor**
	doysh ad*oo*ltoosh poor fav*o*r
Three children, please	**Três crianças, por favor**
[*state price, if there's a choice*]	tresh cree-*a*nsash poor fav*o*r
Stalls/circle/upper circle/sun/ shade	**Plateia/primeiro balcão/segundo balcão/sol/sombra**
	plat*a*y-a/preem*a*y-roo balk*o*wn/ seg*oo*ndoo balk*o*wn/sol/s*a*wmbra
Do you have . . .	**Tem . . .**
	taim . . .
a programme?	**um programa?**
	oom proogr*a*ma
a guide book?	**um guia?**
	oom g*ee*-a
Where's the toilet, please?	**Onde estão os lavabos, por favor?**
	awnd sht*o*wn oosh lav*a*boosh poor fav*o*r
Where's the cloakroom?	**Onde é o vestiário?**
	awnd eh oo veshtee-*a*r-ee-oo

I would like lessons in . . .
Queria lições de . . .
ker*ee*-a lees*oy*nsh der . . .

skiing
esqui
shkee

sailing
vela
v*e*l-a

water skiing
esqui aquático
shkee akw*a*tico

sub-acqua diving
mergulho sub-aquático
meerg*oo*l-yoo soob-akw*a*ticoo

Can I hire . . .
Posso alugar . . .
p*o*ssoo aloog*a*r

some skis?
uns esquis?
*oo*nsh shk*ee*sh

some skiboots?
umas botas de esqui?
*oo*mash b*o*t-ash der shkee

a boat?
um barco?
oom b*a*rcoo

a fishing rod?
uma cana de pesca?
*oo*ma c*a*h-na der p*e*shca

a sun lounger?
um colchão?
oom colsh*ow*n

a beach chair?
uma cadeira de praia?
*oo*ma cad*a*y-ra der pr*a*h-ya

a sun umbrella?
um toldo?
oom t*o*ldoo

the necessary equipment?
o equipamento necessário?
oo eek*ee*pamentoo nessess*a*h-ree-oo

How much is it . . .
Quanto é . . .
kw*a*ntoo eh . . .

per day/per hour?
por dia/por hora?
poor d*ee*-a/poor *o*ra

Do I need a licence?
É preciso ter uma licença?
eh press*ee*zoo tair *oo*ma leess*e*n-sa

Asking if things are allowed

ESSENTIAL INFORMATION

- May one smoke here?
  May we smoke here?
  May I smoke here?
  Can one smoke here?
  Can I smoke here?

  Pode-se fumar aqui?
  pod-ser foom*a*r ak*ee*

- All these English variations can be expressed in one way in Portuguese. To save space, only the first English version (May one . . . ?) is shown below.

WHAT TO SAY

Excuse me, please	**Com licença, por favor** com leessen-sa poor fav*o*r
May one . . .	**Pode-se . . .** pod-ser . . .
camp here?	**acampar aqui?** acamp*a*r ak*ee*
come in?	**entrar?** entr*a*r
dance here?	**dançar aqui?** dans*a*r ak*ee*
fish here?	**pescar aqui?** peshc*a*r ak*ee*
get a drink here?	**comprar uma bebida aqui?** cawmpr*a*r *oo*ma bebeeda ak*ee*
get out this way?	**sair por aqui?** sa-*ee*r poor ak*ee*
get something to eat here?	**comprar algo de comer aqui?** cawmpr*a*r *a*lgoo der coom*ai*r ak*ee*
eat something here?	**comer aqui?** coom*ai*r ak*ee*
leave one's things here?	**deixar as nossas coisas aqui?** day-sh*a*r ash nossash c*o*yzash ak*ee*
look around?	**dar uma vista de olhos?** d*a*r *oo*ma veeshta der *o*l-yoosh
park here?	**estacionar aqui?** shtassee-oon*a*r ak*ee*

May one . . .	**Pode-se . . .**
	pod-ser . . .
picnic here?	**fazer um pique-nique aqui?**
	faz*air* oom *peek-neek* ak*ee*
sit here?	**sentar aqui?**
	sent*ar* ak*ee*
smoke here?	**fumar aqui?**
	foom*ar* ak*ee*
swim here?	**nadar aqui?**
	nad*ar* ak*ee*
telephone here?	**telefonar daqui?**
	telefoon*ar* dak*ee*
take photos here?	**tirar fotos aqui?**
	te*e*rar fotosh ak*ee*
wait here?	**esperar aqui?**
	shper*ar* ak*ee*

LIKELY REACTIONS

Yes, certainly	**Sim, com certeza**
	seem com sert*ez*-a
Help yourself	**Sirva-se**
	s*ee*rva-ser
I think so	**Acho que sim**
	*a*shoo ker seem
Of course	**Pois claro**
	p*o*ysh cl*ar*-oo
Yes, but be careful	**Sim, mas com cuidado**
	seem mash com coo-eed*ah*-doo
No, certainly not	**Não, certamente que não**
	nown sertam*en*t ker nown
I don't think so	**Acho que não**
	*a*shoo ker nown
Not normally	**Normalmente não**
	normalm*en*t nown
Sorry	**Desculpe**
	deshc*oo*lp

Reference

PUBLIC NOTICES

- Key words on signs for drivers, pedestrians, travellers, shoppers and overnight guests.

ATRAVESSE	Cross (the road)
ABERTO	Open
ATENÇÃO	Attention
AVANCE	Go forward
ADMITE-SE PESSOAL	Help wanted
ACENDA AS LUZES	Headlights on
ÁGUA POTÁVEL	Drinking water
ALTO	Halt
ALFÂNDEGA	Customs
ALUGA-SE	To rent
ALUGA-SE QUARTO	Room for rent
ANDAR (PRIMEIRO)	(first) Floor
AUTO-ESTRADA	Highway
ABRANDE	Slow down
AUTOCARRO	Bus
BECO SEM SAÍDA	Dead end
BILHETEIRA	Ticket office
BATER	Knock
BAR	Bar
BERMA PERIGOSA	Dangerous curb
CUIDADO	Caution
CURVA PERIGOSA	Dangerous curve
COMPLETO	Full
CAIS	Platform
CHEGADAS	Arrivals
CASA DE BANHO	Bathroom
CUIDADO COM O CÃO	Beware of the dog
CUIDADO COM O COMBOIO	Beware of trains
CAIXA	Service till
CARRUAGEM RESTAURANTE	Restaurant car
CASA DE JANTAR	Dining room

CONDUZA COM CAUTELA	Drive with caution
CAVALHEIROS	Gentlemen
CENTRO DE INFORMAÇÕES	Information centre
CAVE	Basement
CRUZAMENTO	Crossroads
DEVAGAR	Slow
DÊ PRIORIDADE	Yield
DEPÓSITO DE BAGAGEM	Left luggage
DESVIO	Detour
DUCHE	Shower
ESPERE	Wait
EMPURRE	Push
ESTACIONAMENTO RESERVADO	Parking reserved
ESTACIONAMENTO PROIBIDO	Parking forbidden
ESTRANGULAMENTO	Road narrows
ESCOLA	School
ENTRADA	Entrance
ENTRADA PROIBIDA	No entry
ENTRADA LIVRE	Free entry
ESCADA ROLANTE	Escalator
ELEVADOR	Lift
FOGO	Fire
FIM (DE AUTO-ESTRADA)	End (of highway)
FECHADO	Closed
FRIO	Cold
FUMADORES	Smokers
GADO	Cattle
GADO BRAVO	Wild cattle
GELO	Ice
GUIA	Guide
HOSPITAL	Hospital
HÁ VAGAS	Vacancies
HOMENS	Gentlemen
INÍCIO DE AUTO-ESTRADA	Highway begins
LIMITE DE VELOCIDADE	Speed limit
LOTAÇÃO ESGOTADA	Sold out/full
LUZES	Lights
LUGARES EM PÉ	Standing room
LAVABOS	Toilets

LIVRE	Vacant
LOMBA	Hill
MORTE	Death
METRO	Underground
MIRADOURO	Scenic spot
MANTENHA-SE À DIREITA	Keep right
NÃO MEXER	Do not touch
NÃO POTÁVEL	Not for drinking (water)
OBRAS	Construction
OCUPADO	Occupied
OFERTA ESPECIAL	Special offer
PARAGEM	Stop
PERIGO DE MORTE	Danger of death
PASSAGEM DE NÍVEL	Level crossing
PESADOS (VEÍCULOS)	Heavy (vehicles)
PERIGO	Danger
PARTIDAS	Departures
PARQUE DE ESTACIONAMENTO	Parking
PASSE	Go/cross
PASSAGEM SUBTERRÂNEA	Underground passage
PORTAGEM	Toll
PASSAGEM PROIBIDA A PESSOAS ESTRANHAS AO SERVIÇO	No admittance except for staff
PESSOAL	Staff
PISO ESCORREGADIO	Slippery surface
PARE, ESCUTE, OLHE	Stop, look, listen
POSTO DE SOCORROS	First aid
PERDIDOS E ACHADOS	Lost property
PROIBIDO FUMAR	No smoking
PROIBIDA A ULTRAPASSAGEM	No passing
POLÍCIA	Police
PEÕES	Pedestrians
PORTEIRO	Porter
PRIORIDADE À DIREITA	Priority to the right
PRIVADO	Private
PUXE	Pull
PISO IRREGULAR	Uneven surface
QUEDA DE ROCHAS	Falling rocks
QUEDA DE PEDRAS	Falling stones

QUENTE	Hot
RÉS-DO-CHÃO	Ground floor
RECEPÇÃO	Reception
RESERVAS	Reservations
RESERVADO	Reserved
SALDOS	Sales
SELF-SERVICE	Self-service
SENTIDO ÚNICO	One way
SALA DE ESPERA	Waiting room
SILÊNCIO	Silence
STOP	Stop
SEMÁFOROS	Traffic lights
SERVIÇO	Service
SAÍDA DE EMERGÊNCIA	Emergency exit
SAÍDA DE AUTO-ESTRADA	Highway exit
SAÍDA	Exit/way out
SENHORAS	Ladies
TOQUE	Ring
TRÂNSITO NOS DOIS SENTIDOS	Two-way traffic
TRÂNSITO FECHADO	Traffic closed
VENENO	Poison
VEÍCULOS PESADOS	Heavy vehicles
VIRE À DIREITA/ ESQUERDA	Turn right/left
VENDE-SE	For sale
VELOCIDADE MÁXIMA	Maximum speed
ZONA AZUL	Parking permitted zone

ABBREVIATIONS

(a)	**assinado**	signed by
a/c	**ao cuidado de**	care of
ACP	**Automóvel Club de Portugal**	Portuguese Automobile Club
Apart	**apartamento**	apartment
Arq	**arquitecto**	architect
Av	**avenida**	avenue
c/c	**conta corrente**	current account
Cia	**companhia**	company
CP	**Caminhos de Ferro**	Portuguese railways

2a Cl	**segunda classe**	second class
D., dto.	**direito**	right
Dr	**doutor**	doctor
End. Tel.	**endereço telegráfico**	telegraph address
EUA	**Estados Unidos da América**	USA
Ex.mo Sr	**Excelentíssimo senhor**	Dear sir
Esc.	**escudo**	escudo
E.,esq.	**esquerdo**	left
GNR	**Guarda Nacional Republicana**	National Guard
Gov	**governo**	government
Kg	**quilo**	kilo
L	**litro**	litre
N°	**número**	number
L	**largo**	square
M	**metro**	underground
NªSra	**Nossa Senhora**	Our Lady
N°Sr	**Nosso Senhor**	Our Lord
P	**praça**	square
Pág	**página**	page
Ps	**peso**	weight
R	**rua**	street
r/c	**rés-do-chão**	ground floor
Reg	**registado**	registered
Reg.to	**regulamento**	rule
Rem	**remetente**	sender
SARL	**Sociedade Anónima de Responsabilidade Limitada**	limited company
SFF	**se faz favor**	please
S, Sto, Sta	**São, santo, santa**	saint
Sr	**senhor**	Mr
Sra	**senhora**	Mrs
Tel	**telefone**	telephone

NUMBERS
Cardinal numbers

0	**zero**	zeh-roo
1	**um**	oom
2	**dois**	doysh
3	**três**	tresh
4	**quatro**	kwatroo
5	**cinco**	seencoo
6	**seis**	saysh
7	**sete**	set
8	**oito**	oytoo
9	**nove**	nov
10	**dez**	desh
11	**onze**	awnz
12	**doze**	dawz
13	**treze**	trez
14	**catorze**	catorz
15	**quinze**	keenz
16	**dezasseis**	dez-asaysh
17	**dezassete**	dez-aset
18	**dezoito**	dez-oytoo
19	**dezanove**	dez-anov
20	**vinte**	veent
21	**vinte e um**	veent ee oom
22	**vinte e dois**	veent ee doysh
23	**vinte e três**	veent ee tresh
24	**vinte e quatro**	veent ee kwatroo
25	**vinte e cinco**	veent ee seencoo
26	**vinte e seis**	veent ee saysh
27	**vinte e sete**	veent ee set
28	**vinte e oito**	veent ee oytoo
29	**vinte e nove**	veent ee nov
30	**trinta**	treenta
31	**trinta e um**	treenta ee oom
32	**trinta e dois**	treenta ee doysh
33	**trinta e três**	treenta ee tresh
34	**trinta e quatro**	treenta ee kwatroo
35	**trinta e cinco**	treenta ee seencoo
40	**quarenta**	kwarenta
41	**quarenta e um**	kwarenta ee oom
45	**quarenta e cinco**	kwarenta ee seencoo

50	**cinquenta**	seenkwenta
55	**cinquenta e cinco**	seenkwenta ee seencoo
60	**sessenta**	sessenta
66	**sessenta e seis**	sessenta ee saysh
70	**setenta**	set-enta
77	**setenta e sete**	set-enta ee set
80	**oitenta**	oytenta
88	**oitenta e oito**	oytenta ee oytoo
90	**noventa**	nooventa
99	**noventa e nove**	nooventa ee nov
100	**cem**	saim
101	**cento e um**	sentoo ee oom
102	**cento e dois**	sentoo ee doysh
125	**cento e vinte cinco**	sentoo ee veent ee seencoo
150	**cento e cinquenta**	sentoo ee seenkwenta
175	**cento e setenta e cinco**	sentoo ee set-enta ee seencoo
200	**duzentos**	doozentoosh
300	**trezentos**	trez-entoosh
400	**quatrocentos**	kwatrosentoosh
500	**quinhentos**	keen-yentoosh
1,000	**mil**	meel
2,000	**dois mil**	doysh meel
10,000	**dez mil**	desh meel
100,000	**cem mil**	saim meel
1,000,000	**um milhão**	oom meel-yown

Ordinal numbers

1st	**primeiro (1°)**	preemay-roo
2nd	**segundo (2°)**	segoondoo
3rd	**terceiro (3°)**	tersay-roo
4th	**quarto (4°)**	kwartoo
5th	**quinto (4°)**	keentoo
6th	**sexto (6°)**	sayshtoo
7th	**sétimo (7°)**	set-eemoo
8th	**oitavo (8°)**	oytavoo
9th	**nono (9°)**	nawnoo
10th	**décimo (10°)**	desseemoo
11th	**décimo primeiro (11°)**	desseemoo preemay-roo
12th	**décimo segundo (12°)**	desseemoo segoondoo

TIME

What time is it?	**Que horas são?**
	ker *o*rash sown
It's one o'clock	**É uma hora**
	eh *oo*ma *o*ra
It's . . .	**São . . .**
	sown . . .
two o'clock	**duas horas**
	d*oo*-ash *o*rash
three o'clock	**três horas**
	tresh *o*rash
four o'clock	**quatro horas**
	kw*a*troo *o*rash
in the morning	**da manhã**
	da man-y*a*n
in the afternoon	**da tarde**
	da tard
at night	**da noite**
	da noyt
It's . . .	**É . . .**
	eh . . .
noon	**meio-dia**
	m*a*y-oo d*ee*-a
midnight	**meia-noite**
	m*a*y-a noyt
It's . . .	**São . . .**
	sown . . .
five past five	**cinco e cinco**
	s*ee*ncoo ee s*ee*ncoo
ten past five	**cinco e dez**
	s*ee*ncoo ee desh
a quarter past five	**cinco e um quarto**
	s*ee*ncoo ee oom kw*a*rtoo
twenty past five	**cinco e vinte**
	s*ee*ncoo ee veent
twenty five past five	**cinco e vinte cinco**
	s*ee*ncoo ee veent s*ee*ncoo
half past five	**cinco e meia**
	s*ee*ncoo ee m*a*y-a
twenty five to six	**vinte e cinco para as seis**
	veent ee s*ee*ncoo p*a*ra as saysh
twenty to six	**vinte para as seis**
	veent p*a*ra ash saysh

a quarter to six	**um quarto para as seis**
	oom kwartoo para ash saysh
ten to six	**dez para as seis**
	desh para ash saysh
five to six	**cinco para as seis**
	seencoo para ash saysh
At what times (does the train leave)?	**A que horas (parte o comboio)?**
	a ker orash (part oo comboy-oo)
At . . .	**Às . . .**
	ash . . .
13.00	**treze**
	trez
14.05	**catorze e cinco**
	catorz ee seencoo
15.10	**quinze e dez**
	keenz ee desh
16.15	**dezasseis e quinze**
	dez-asaysh ee keenz
17.20	**dezassete e vinte**
	dez-aset ee veent
18.25	**dezoito e vinte cinco**
	dez-oytoo ee veent seencoo
19.30	**dezanove e trinta**
	dez-anov ee treenta
20.35	**vinte e trinta e cinco**
	veent ee treenta ee seencoo
21.40	**vinte e uma e quarenta**
	veent ee ooma ee kwarenta
22.45	**vinte e duas e quarenta e cinco**
	veent ee doo-ash ee kwarenta ee seencoo
23.50	**vinte e três e cinquenta**
	veent ee tresh ee seenkwenta
0.55	**zero e cinquenta e cinco**
	zeh-roo ee seenkwenta ee seencoo
in ten minutes	**dentro de dez minutos**
	dentroo der desh meenootoosh
in a quarter of an hour	**daqui a um quarto de hora**
	dakee a oom kwartoo der ora
in half an hour	**dentro de meia hora**
	dentroo der may-a ora
in three quarters of an hour	**daqui a três quartos de hora**
	dakee a tresh kwartoosh der ora

DAYS

Monday	**segunda-feira**
	seg*oo*nda f*a*yra
Tuesday	**terça-feira**
	t*ai*rsa f*a*yra
Wednesday	**quarta-feira**
	kw*a*rta f*a*yra
Thursday	**quinta-feira**
	k*ee*nta f*a*yra
Friday	**sexta-feira**
	s*a*yshta f*a*yra
Saturday	**sábado**
	s*a*b-adoo
Sunday	**domingo**
	doom*ee*ngoo
last Monday	**segunda-feira passada**
	seg*oo*nda f*a*yra pass*ah*-da
next Tuesday	**na próxima terça-feira**
	na pr*o*sseema t*ai*rsa f*a*yra
on Wednesday	**na quarta-feira**
	na kw*a*rta f*a*yra
on Thursdays	**às quintas-feiras**
	*a*sh k*ee*ntash f*a*yrash
until Friday	**até sexta-feira**
	at*eh* s*a*yshta f*a*yra
before Saturday	**antes de sábado**
	*a*ntesh der s*a*b-adoo
after Sunday	**depois de domingo**
	dep*oy*sh der doom*ee*ngoo
the day before yesterday	**anteontem**
	antee-*a*wntaim
two days ago	**há dois dias**
	ah doysh d*ee*e-ash
yesterday	**ontem**
	*a*wntaim
yesterday morning	**ontem de manhã**
	*a*wntaim der man-y*a*n
yesterday afternoon	**ontem à tarde**
	*a*wntaim ah tard
last night	**ontem à noite**
	*a*wntaim ah noyt

today	**hoje**
	awj
this morning	**esta manhã**
	*e*shta man-y*a*n
this afternoon	**esta tarde**
	*e*shta tard
tonight	**esta noite**
	*e*shta noyt
tomorrow	**amanhã**
	aman-y*a*n
tomorrow morning	**amanhã de manhã**
	aman-y*a*n der man-y*a*n
tomorrow afternoon	**amanhã à tarde**
	aman-y*a*n ah tard
tomorrow evening	**amanhã ao fim da tarde**
	aman-y*a*n *a*h-oo feem da tard
tomorrow night	**amanhã à noite**
	aman-y*a*n ah noyt
the day after tomorrow	**depois de amanhã**
	dep*o*ysh der aman-y*a*n

MONTHS AND DATES

January	**Janeiro**
	jan*ay*-roo
February	**Fevereiro**
	fev-e*ray*-roo
March	**Março**
	m*ar*soo
April	**Abril**
	abr*eel*
May	**Maio**
	m*ah*-ee-oo
June	**Junho**
	j*oon*-yoo
July	**Julho**
	j*ool*-yoo
August	**Agosto**
	ag*aw*shtoo
September	**Setembro**
	set-*embro*o
October	**Outubro**
	awt*oo*broo
November	**Novembro**
	noov*em*broo
December	**Dezembro**
	dez-*embro*o
in January	**em Janeiro**
	aim jan*ay*-roo
until February	**até Fevereiro**
	at*eh* fev-e*ray*-roo
before March	**antes de Março**
	antsh der m*ar*soo
after April	**depois de Abril**
	depoysh der abr*eel*
during May	**durante Maio**
	door*ant* m*ah*-ee-oo
not until June	**não antes de Junho**
	nown antsh der j*oon*-yoo
the beginning of July	**o princípio de Julho**
	oo preens*eepee*-oo der j*ool*-yoo
the middle of August	**o meio de Agosto**
	oo m*ay*-oo der ag*aw*shtoo

the end of September	**o fim de Setembro**
	oo feem der setembroo
last month	**o mês passado**
	oo mesh passah-doo
this month	**este mês**
	esht mesh
next month	**o próximo mês**
	oo prosseemoo mesh
in spring	**na primavera**
	na preemavera
in summer	**no verão**
	noo verown
in autumn	**no outono**
	noo awtawnoo
in winter	**no inverno**
	noo eenvernoo
this year	**este ano**
	esht an-oo
last year	**o ano passado**
	oo an-oo passah-doo
next year	**o próximo ano**
	oo prosseemoo an-oo
in 1982	**em mil novecentos e oitenta e dois**
	aim meel nov-sentoosh ee oytenta ee doysh
in 1985	**em mil novecentos e oitenta e cinco**
	aim meel nov-sentoosh ee oytenta ee seenco
in 1990	**em mil novecentos e noventa**
	aim meel nov-sentoosh ee nooventa
What's the date today?	**Qual é a data de hoje?**
	kwal eh a dah-ta der awj
It's the 6th of March	**Seis de Março**
	saysh der marsoo
It's the 12th of April	**Doze de Abril**
	dawz der abreel
It's the 21st of August	**Vinte e um de Agosto**
	veent ee oom der agawshtoo

Public holidays

- Offices, shops and schools are all closed on the following dates.
  Each city also has its own public holiday: check with the tourist
  office here for dates.

1 January	**Ano Novo**	New Year's Day
. . .	**Sexta Feira Santa**	Good Friday
25 April	**Vinte e cinco de Abril**	Freedom Day (date of 1974 revolution)
1 May	**Dia do Trabalhador**	Labour Day
. . .	**Corpo de Deus**	Corpus Christi
10 June	**Dia de Portugal**	National Day
15 August	**Assunção**	Assumption Day
5 October	**Proclamação da Replíca**	Proclamation of the Republic
1 November	**Todos os Santos**	All Saints' Day
1 December	**Restauração da Independência**	Restoration of Independence
8 December	**Imaculada Conceição**	Immaculate Conception
25 December	**Natal**	Christmas Day

COUNTRIES AND NATIONALITIES
Countries

Australia	**Austrália** ah-oosh-trahlia
Austria	**Áustria** ah-ooshtria
Belgium	**Bélgica** beljeeca
Britain	**Grã-Bretanha** gran-bretan-ya
Canada	**Canadá** canadah
East Africa	**África de Leste** africa der lesht
Eire	**Irlanda do Sul** eerlanda doo sool
England	**Inglaterra** eenglatairra
France	**França** franssa

Greece	**Grécia**
	gressia
India	**Índia**
	*ee*ndia
Italy	**Itália**
	eet*a*l-ee-a
Luxembourg	**Luxemburgo**
	looshem-b*oo*rgoo
Netherlands	**Holanda**
	*o*l-anda
New Zealand	**Nova Zelândia**
	nova zel*a*ndia
Northern Ireland	**Irlanda do Norte**
	eerl*a*nda doo nort
Pakistan	**Paquistão**
	pakeesh-t*o*wn
Portugal	**Portugal**
	poortoog*a*l
Scotland	**Escócia**
	shkossia
South Africa	**África do Sul**
	*a*frica doo sool
Spain	**Espanha**
	shp*a*n-ya
Switzerland	**Suíça**
	soo-*ee*ssa
United States	**Estados Unidos**
	sht*a*h-doosh oon*ee*doosh
Wales	**País de Gales**
	pa-*ee*sh der galsh
West Germany	**Alemanha Ocidental**
	al-eman-ya osseedent*a*l

Examples

These (letters) are for England	**Estas (cartas) são para Inglaterra**
	*e*shtash (c*a*rtash) sown p*a*ra eenglat*a*irra
I'd like this number in Ireland	**Queria este número na Irlanda**
	ker*ee*-a esht n*oo*meroo na eerl*a*nda

Nationalities
[*Use the first alternative for men, the second for women*]

American	**americano/a**
	america*noo*/a
Australian	**australiano/a**
	*a*h-ooshtralee-*a*n-oo/a
British	**britânico/a**
	breet*a*nicoo/a
Canadian	**canadiano/a**
	canadee-*a*n-oo/a
East African	**africano/a de leste**
	african-oo/a der lesht
English	**inglês/inglesa**
	eengl*e*sh/eengl*e*z-a
Indian	**indiano/a**
	eendee-*a*n-oo/a
Irish	**irlandês/irlandesa**
	eerland*e*sh/eerland*e*z-a
New Zealander	**neo zelandês/zelandesa**
	n*e*h-o zeland*e*sh/zeland*e*z-a
Pakistani	**paquistanês/paquistanesa**
	pakeeshtan*e*sh/pakeeshtan*e*z-a
Scots	**escocês/escocesa**
	shkoos*e*sh/shkoos*e*z-a
South African	**sul africano/a**
	sool african-oo/a
Welsh	**galês/galesa**
	gal*e*sh/gal*e*z-a

DEPARTMENT STORE GUIDE

Almofadas	Cushions
Andar	Floor
Artigos de viagem	Travel goods
Artigos regionais	Local crafts
Barros	Pottery
Bébés	Babywear
Blusas	Blouses
Brinquedos	Toys
Cabedais	Leathers
Camas	Beds
Camisaria	Shirt department
Camisas	Shirts
Camisolas	Jumpers
Camping	Camping
Capelista	Haberdashery
Cave	Basement
Chapelaria	Millinery department
Chinelos	Slippers
Cintas	Corsets
Cintos	Belts
Cobertores	Blankets
Contas	Accounts
Cortinados	Curtains
Crianças	Children's department
Cutelaria	Cutlery
Discos	Records
Electro-domésticos	Electrical appliances
Espelhos	Mirrors
Faiança	China
Ferragens	Hardware
Fotografia	Photographic department
Gravatas	Ties
Homens	Gentlemen
Informações	Information
Jóias	Jewellery
Livros	Books
Loiça	Crockery
Luvas	Gloves
Mercearia	Grocery department
Mobília	Furniture

Mobiliário caseiro	Home furnishings
Modas para senhora	Ladies' fashions
Móveis de cozinha	Kitchen furniture
Papelaria	Stationery
Perfumaria	Perfumery
Peúgas	Socks
Prendas	Gifts
Presentes	Gifts
Primeiro	First
Produtos alimentares	Food department
Produtos de beleza	Beauty products
Produtos de limpeza	Cleaning products
Pronto a vestir	Ready-to-wear
Quarto	Fourth
Rádios	Radios
Rés-do-chão	Ground floor
Roupa de cama	Bed linen
Roupa interior	Underwear
Segundo	Second
Soutiens	Bras
Sapateiro	Heel bar
Sapatos	Shoes
Senhoras	Ladies
Tapetes	Rugs
Tecidos	Fabrics
Tecidos de vestir	Dress fabrics
Televisões	Televisions
Toalhas	Towels
Vidros	Glass

CONVERSION TABLES

Read the centre column of these tables from right to left to convert from metric to imperial and from left to right to convert from imperial to metric e.g. 5 litres = 8.80 pints; 5 pints = 2.84 litres

pints		litres		gallons		litres
1.76	1	0.57		0.22	1	4.55
3.52	2	1.14		0.44	2	9.09
5.28	3	1.70		0.66	3	13.64
7.07	4	2.27		0.88	4	18.18
8.80	5	2.84		1.00	5	22.73
10.56	6	3.41		1.32	6	27.28
12.32	7	3.98		1.54	7	31.82
14.08	8	4.55		1.76	8	36.37
15.84	9	5.11		1.98	9	40.91

ounces		grams		pounds		kilos
0.04	1	28.35		2.20	1	0.45
0.07	2	56.70		4.41	2	0.91
0.11	3	85.05		6.61	3	1.36
0.14	4	113.40		8.82	4	1.81
0.18	5	141.75		11.02	5	2.27
0.21	6	170.10		13.23	6	2.72
0.25	7	198.45		15.43	7	3.18
0.28	8	226.80		17.64	8	3.63
0.32	9	255.15		19.84	9	4.08

inches		centimetres		yards		metres
0.39	1	2.54		1.09	1	0.91
0.79	2	5.08		2.19	2	1.83
1.18	3	7.62		3.28	3	2.74
1.58	4	10.16		4.37	4	3.66
1.95	5	12.70		5.47	5	4.57
2.36	6	15.24		6.56	6	5.49
2.76	7	17.78		7.66	7	6.40
3.15	8	20.32		8.65	8	7.32
3.54	9	22.86		9.84	9	8.23

miles		kilometres
0.62	1	1.61
1.24	2	3.22
1.86	3	4.83
2.49	4	6.44
3.11	5	8.05
3.73	6	9.66
4.35	7	11.27
4.97	8	12.87
5.59	9	14.48

A quick way to convert kilometres to miles: divide by 8 and multiply by 5. To convert miles to kilometres: divide by 5 and multiply by 8.

fahrenheit (°F)	centigrade (°C)		lbs/ sq in	k/ sq cm
212°	100°	boiling point	18	1.3
100°	38°		20	1.4
98.4°	36.9°	body temperature	22	1.5
86°	30°		25	1.7
77°	25°		29	2.0
68°	20°		32	2.3
59°	15°		35	2.5
50°	10°		36	2.5
41°	5°		39	2.7
32°	0°	freezing point	40	2.8
14°	−10°		43	3.0
−4°	−20°		45	3.2
			46	3.2
			50	3.5
			60	4.2

To convert °C to °F, divide by 5, multiply by 9 and add 32. To convert °F to °C, take away 32, divide by 9 and multiply by 5.

CLOTHING SIZES

Remember – always try on clothes before buying. Clothing sizes are usually unreliable.

Women's dresses and suits

Europe	38	40	42	44	46	48
UK	32	34	36	38	40	42
USA	10	12	14	16	18	20

men's suits and coats

Europe	46	48	50	52	54	56
UK and USA	36	38	40	42	44	46

men's shirts

Europe	36	37	38	39	41	42	43
UK and USA	14	14½	15	15½	16	16½	17

socks

Europe	38–39	39–40	40–41	41–42	42–43
UK and USA	9½	10	10½	11	11½

shoes

Europe	34	35½	36½	38	39	41	42	43	44	45
UK	2	3	4	5	6	7	8	9	10	11
USA	3½	4½	5½	6½	7½	8½	9½	10½	11½	12½

Do it yourself

Some notes on the language

This section does not deal with 'grammar' as such. The purpose here is to explain some of the most obvious and elementary nuts and bolts of the language, based on the principal phrases included in the book. This information should enable you to produce numerous sentences of your own making, although you will obviously still be fairly limited in what you can say.

There is no pronunciation guide in the first part of this section, partly because it would get in the way of the explanations and partly because you have to do it yourself at this stage if you are serious – work out the pronunciation from all the earlier examples in the book.

THE

All nouns in Portuguese belong to one of two genders: masculine or feminine, irrespective of whether they refer to living beings or inanimate objects.

The (singular)	masculine	feminine
the address		**a morada**
the apple		**a maçã**
the bill		**a conta**
the cup of tea		**a chávena de chá**
the glass of wine	**o copo de vinho**	
the key		**a chave**
the luggage		**a bagagem**
the menu	**o menu**	
the newspaper	**o jornal**	
the receipt	**o recibo**	
the sandwich		**a sandes**
the suitcase		**a mala**
the telephone directory		**a lista telefónica**
the timetable	**o horário**	

Important things to remember

- You can often tell if a singular noun is masculine or feminine by its ending. Masculine nouns usually end in **o** and feminine nouns in **a**. However, there are several exceptions to this basic rule and there are many groups of nouns ending in **e, l, z** and others, so you should try to learn and remember all genders. If you are reading a word with **o** or **a** in front of it, you can detect its gender immediately: **o horário** is masculine (*m.* in dictionaries) and **a morada** is feminine (*f.* in dictionaries).
- *The* is **o** before a masculine noun and **a** before a feminine noun.
- Does it matter? Not unless you want to make a serious attempt to speak correctly and scratch beneath the surface of the language. You would be understood if you said **a horário** or **o morada**, providing your pronunciation was good.

The (plural)	masculine	feminine
the addresses		**as moradas**
the apples		**as maçãs**
the bills		**as contas**
the cups of tea		**as chávenas de chá**
the glasses of wine	**os copos de vinho**	
the keys		**as chaves**
the luggage	(*this is only singular in Portuguese, see above*)	
the menus	**os menus**	
the newspapers	**os jornais**	
the receipts	**os recibos**	
the sandwiches		**as sandes**
the suitcases		**as malas**
the telephone directories		**as listas telefónicas**
the timetables	**os horários**	

Important things to remember

- As a general rule, a noun ending in a vowel adds an **s** to become plural; a noun ending in a consonant, such as **r** or **z**, adds **es** to become plural; a noun ending in **l** changes to **is** to become plural. But watch out for the many exceptions.
- *The* is **os** before a plural masculine noun and **as** before a plural feminine noun.

Look at the list below:

the beer	**a cerveja**	some beer	**cerveja**
the bread	**o pão**	some bread	**pão**
the butter	**a manteiga**	some butter	**manteiga**
the cheese	**o queijo**	some cheese	**queijo**

The same would apply to the following words:

the coffee	**o café**	the sugar	**o açúcar**
the flour	**a farinha**	the tea	**o chá**
the lemonade	**a limonada**	the water	**a água**
the olive oil	**o azeite**	the wine	**o vinho**

Practice saying and writing these sentences in Portuguese: note that there are two ways of saying *Have you got?* politely, in Portuguese; **tem** (when speaking to one person). **têm** (when speaking to more than one person or in an 'organization' – e.g. a hotel, a shop or a tourist information office).

Have you got some coffee?	**Tem café?**
Have you got some flour?	
Have you got some sugar?	
I'd like some butter	**Queria manteiga**
I'd like some olive oil	
I'd like some bread	
Is there any lemonade?	**Há limonada?**
Is there any water?	
Is there any wine?	
Where can I get some cheese?	**Onde posso obter queijo?**
Where can I get some flour?	
Where can I get some wine?	
I'll have some beer	**Queria cerveja**
I'll have some tea	
I'll have some coffee	
Have you got the key?	**Tem a chave?**
Have you got the timetable?	**Têm o horário?**
Have you got the menu?	**Tem o menu?**
Have you got the receipt?	**Tem o recibo?**
Where is the key?	**Onde está a chave?**
Where is the timetable?	**Onde . . . ?**
Where is the address?	

Where is the suitcase?
Where are the keys?   **Onde estão as chaves?**
Where are the suitcases?   **Onde estão . . . ?**
Where are the apples?
Where are the timetables?
Where can I get the key?   **Onde posso obter a chave?**
Where can I get the address?   **Onde posso obter . . . ?**
Where can I get the
  timetables?

Now make up more sentences along the same lines.
Try adding please: **por favor**, at the end.

A/AN

A/an (singular)	masculine	feminine
an address		uma morada
an apple		uma maçã
a bill		uma conta
a cup of tea		uma chávena de chá
a glass of beer	um copo de cerveja	
a key		uma chave
a menu	um menu	
a newspaper	um jornal	
a sandwich		uma sandes
a suitcase		uma mala
a telephone directory		uma lista telefónica
a timetable	um horário	

Important things to remember

1. *A* or *an* is **um** before masculine nouns and **uma** before feminine nouns.
2. The plural, *some* or *any* is **uns** before masculine nouns and **umas** before feminine nouns.
3. In certain Portuguese expressions, **uns** and **umas** are left out. See examples of this in the sentences marked * below.

some/any (plural)	masculine	feminine
addresses		umas moradas
apples		umas maçãs
bills		umas contas
cups of tea		umas chávenas de chá
glasses of wine	uns copos de vinho	
keys		umas chaves
menus	uns menus	
newspapers	uns jornais	
receipts	uns recibos	
sandwiches		umas sandes
suitcases		umas malas
telephone directories		umas listas telefónicas
timetables	uns horários	

Practise writing and saying these sentences in Portuguese:

Have you got a receipt?	**Tem um recibo?**
Have you got a menu?	
I'd like a telephone directory	**Queria uma lista telefónica**
I'd like some sandwiches	
Where can I get some newspapers?	***Onde posso obter jornais?**
Where can I get a cup of tea?	
Is there a key?	**Há uma chave?**
Is there a timetable?	
Are there any keys?	***Há chaves?**
Are there any newspapers?	

Now make up more sentences along the same lines.

Then try these new phrases:

Queria . . . (I'll have . . .)
Preciso de . . . (I need . . .)

I'll have a glass of wine	**Queria um copo de vinho**
I'll have some sandwiches	**Queria . . .**
I'll have some apples	
I need a cup of tea	**Preciso de uma chávena de chá**
I need a key	**Preciso de . . .**
	Note that **de uma** is usually spelt **duma; de um, dum; de umas, dumas** and **de uns, duns.**
I need some addresses	***Preciso de moradas**
I need some suitcases	***Preciso de . . .**

SOME/ANY

In cases where *some* or *any* refer to more than one thing, such as *some/any ice-creams* and *some/any apples*, **ums** and **umas** are used as explained earlier:
uns gelados (some/any ice-creams)
umas maçãs (some/any apples)
As a guide, you can usually *count* the number of containers or whole items.
In cases where *some* refers to part of a whole thing or an indefinite quantity in English, there is no Portuguese equivalent. Just leave it out. (See the examples on p. 145)

THIS AND THAT

There are two words in Portuguese
isto (this)
aquilo (that)
If you don't know the Portuguese for an object, just point and say:
Queria aquilo ⎡I'd like that
⎣I'll have that
Preciso de isto I need this
Note that **de isto** is usually spelt **disto; de aquilo, daquilo.**

HELPING OTHERS

You can help yourself with phrases such as:

I'd like . . . a sandwich	**Queria . . . uma sandes**
Where can I get . . . a cup of tea?	**Onde posso obter . . . uma chávena de chá?**
I'll have . . . a glass of wine	**Queria . . . um copo de vinho**
I need . . . a receipt	**Preciso de . . . um recibo**

If you come across a compatriot having trouble making himself or herself understood, you should be able to speak to the Portuguese person on their behalf.

Note that it is not necessary to say the words for *he* (**ele**), *she* (**ela**) and *I* (**eu**) in Portuguese unless you what to emphasize them, e.g.:
He'll have a beer and *I'll* have a glass of wine.

A pronunciation guide is provided from here on.

He'd like . . .	**(Ele) queria uma sandes**
	(el) ker*ee*-a *oo*ma sandsh
She'd like . . .	**(Ela) queria uma sandes**
	(el-a) ker*ee*-a *oo*ma sandsh
Where can he get . . . ?	**Onde pode obter uma chávena de chá?**
	awnd pod *o*btair *oo*ma shah-vna der shah
Where can she get . . . ?	**Onde pode obter uma chávena de chá?**
	awnd pod *o*btair *oo*ma shah-vna der shah
He needs . . .	**(Ele) precisa dum recibo**
	(el) press*ee*za doom res*ee*boo
She needs . . .	**(Ela) precisa dum recibo**
	(el-a) press*ee*za doom res*ee*boo

You can also help a couple or a group if they are having difficulties. The Portuguese word for *they* is **eles** (men) and **elas** (women), and **eles** (men and women) but it is usually left out altogether. Look at the verb ending:

They'd like . . .	**(Eles) queriam queijo** (el-esh) ker*ee*-awn c*a*y-joo **(Elas) queriam queijo** (*e*l-ash) ker*ee*-awn c*a*y-joo
Where can they get . . . ?	**Onde podem obter manteiga?** awnd pod-aim *o*btair mant*a*y-ga
They'll have . . .	**Queriam vinho** ker*ee*-awn v*ee*n-yoo
They need . . .	**Precisam de água** press*ee*zawn der *a*h-gwa

What about the two of you? No problem. The word for *we* is **nós**, but it is only really important to change the verb ending.

We'd like . . .	**Queríamos vinho** ker*ee*am-oosh v*ee*n-yoo
Where can we get . . . ?	**Onde podemos obter água?** awnd p*oo*dem-oosh *o*btair *a*h-gwa
We'll have . . .	**Queríamos cerveja** ker*ee*am-oosh serv*a*y-ja
We need . .	**Precisamos de açúcar** press*ee*zam-oosh der ass*oo*-car

Try writing your own checklist for these four useful phrase-starters, like this:

Queria . . .	**Queríamos . . .**
(Ele) queria . . .	**(Eles) queriam . . .**
(Ela) queria . . .	**(Elas) queriam . . .**
Onde posso obter . . . ?	**Onde podemos obter . . . ?**
Onde pode (ele) obter . . . ?	**Onde podem (eles) obter . . . ?**
Onde pode (ela) obter . . . ?	**Onde podem (elas) obter . . . ?**

MORE PRACTICE

Here are some more Portuguese names of things. See how many different sentences you can make up, using the various points of information given earlier in this section.

		singular	plural
1	ashtray	cinzeiro (*m*)	cinzeiros
2	bag	saco (*m*)	sacos
3	car	carro (*m*)	carros
4	cigarette	cigarro (*m*)	cigarros
5	corkscrew	saca rolhas (*m*)	saca rolhas
6	garage	garagem (*f*)	garagens
7	grape	uva (*f*)	uvas
8	ice-cream	gelado (*m*)	gelados
9	knife	faca (*f*)	facas
10	melon	melão (*m*)	melões
11	passport	passaporte (*m*)	passaportes
12	postcard	postal (*m*)	postais
13	salad	salada (*f*)	saladas
14	shoe	sapato (*m*)	sapatos
15	stamp	selo (*m*)	selos
16	station	estação (*f*)	estações
17	street	rua (*f*)	ruas
18	sunglasses	óculos de sol (*m*)	óculos de sol
19	telephone	telefone (*m*)	telefones
20	ticket	bilhete (*m*)	bilhetes

Index